Presenting Numbers, Tables, and Charts

Sally Bigwood is a trainer and consultant specializing in presenting numeric information. She has over twenty years' experience as a researcher and corporate planner in the public sector as well as having private-sector experience in the UK and the United States. She and Melissa Spore are sisters.

Melissa Spore is an instructional designer with extensive experience of developing educational materials for print, television, and the Internet. She has a special interest in improving student writing through technology and in document design for print and online. She is a member of the faculty of the University of Saskatchewan, Canada.

One Step Ahead . . .

The *One Step Ahead* series is for all those who want and need to communicate more effectively in a range of real-life situations. Each title provides up-to-date practical guidance, tips, and the language tools to enhance your writing and speaking.

Series Editor: John Seely

Acknowledgements

Many people have contributed to the writing of this book. In particular the authors would like to thank Professor A. S. C. Ehrenberg, Professor Martin Collins, and Dr John Bound for their generous time and useful criticisms. This book could not have been written without the work of Professor Edward R. Tufte and Myra Chapman. We would also like to thank Neil Bendel, Morna Greuel, Heather McWhinney, Perry Millar, Dr Earl Misanchuk, Mel Powell, and David Singer.

This book is dedicated to our parents.

Presenting Numbers, Tables, and Charts

Sally Bigwood and Melissa Spore

Cartoons by Beatrice Baumgartner-Cohen

OXFORD
UNIVERSITY PRESS

OXFORD UNIVERSITY PRESS

Great Clarendon Street, Oxford OX2 6DP

Oxford University Press is a department of the University of Oxford.
It furthers the University's objective of excellence in research, scholarship,
and education by publishing worldwide in
Oxford New York
Auckland Bangkok Buenos Aires Cape Town Chennai
Dar es Salaam Delhi Hong Kong Istanbul Karachi Kolkata
Kuala Lumpur Madrid Melbourne Mexico City Mumbai Nairobi
São Paulo Shanghai Taipei Tokyo Toronto

Oxford is a registered trade mark of Oxford University Press
in the UK and in certain other countries

Published in the United States
by Oxford University Press Inc., New York

British Library Cataloguing in Publication Data
Data available

Library of Congress Cataloging in Publication Data
Data available

ISBN 0-19-860722-9

10 9 8 7 6 5 4 3 2 1

Typeset by Footnote Graphics Ltd, Warminster, Wiltshire
Printed by Giunti Industrie Grafiche Prato, Italy

Contents

1 Introduction

*Statistical
thinking will one
day be as
necessary a
qualification for
efficient
citizenship as the
ability to read
and write.*

H.G. Wells

Numbers are exciting. They tell a story. The trick is to know what story you want to tell and to tell it clearly.

This book is not about how to use a spreadsheet, how to choose the most appropriate statistical technique, or how to manage software. Instead, it gives advice on the simple steps it takes to transform data into readable, relevant information. It is about how to communicate numbers to other people.

Simple guidelines for presenting figures, tables, and graphs have been established over the past thirty years, but few people are aware of them. This book draws together these principles and explains the straightforward steps to make your tables and graphs meaningful.

A communication skill

There are a number of reasons why presenting numerical information is a key communication skill for the 21st century:

■ People find numbers persuasive. Numbers provide sound evidence for many decisions in life, from buying a car to government investment in health care or the military.

■ User-friendly tables, graphs, and numbers can shorten meetings, save time, and make a good impression. In the same way that everyone appreciates well-written, concise reports, people also appreciate the clear, succinct use of numeric information.

- Poor presentation leads to poor decision-making. We will never know the amount of time or money lost through misunderstanding or misinterpreting badly presented figures.

- Most tables and graphs require only arithmetic to be understood. This means that well-designed tables and graphs can communicate nearly all numeric information to the public.

- Tables and graphs are now prevalent thanks to the increased use of computers. Communicating numeric information with ease and confidence will increasingly be an advantage in society.

Many highly numerate professionals—accountants, engineers, and economists—communicate numbers poorly. Like most people, they need to learn the easy steps to communicating data to their audience.

The Challenger tragedy

The 1986 explosion of the Challenger space shuttle, in which seven astronauts died, is the most famous example of poor numerical communication. The evening before take-off, engineers recommended NASA cancel the launch because unexpectedly cold weather could damage some parts. Their hastily composed graphs focused on selective information (the effect of falling temperatures) and omitted equivalent data. NASA found the argument unconvincing and the rocket was launched, exploding after 73 seconds. A full explanation of the graphs and decisions is found in Edward R. Tufte's book *Visual Explanations*.

CAMPAIGN AGAINST CHART JUNK

Improving standards

There are simple steps you can take to improve standards about the presentation of numbers. We suggest you:

- learn and use the simple principles of presenting tables and graphs clearly, as explained in this book.

- try to see your tables and graphs from the audience's point of view. Will they understand your message from the way you have shown it? Will they be persuaded by your use of numbers?

■ appreciate that numbers, like words, can be communicated well or badly. Given a choice, most of us would prefer to communicate well.

■ complain when you see confusing tables and graphs. Play a part in trying to improve standards. If you cannot decipher a table or graph without extensive effort, complain. Suggest that the problem may be with the presentation, not your mathematics.

■ recommend your organization or workplace adopt standards for presenting numeric information.

The chapters

The chapters in this book are set out as follows:

Chapter 2, 'Handling numbers', lays out principles for presenting numeric information. These ideas are basic to good communication. It includes a guide to rounding numbers.

Chapter 3, 'Using tables', makes detailed recommendations for table construction and discusses reference and demonstration tables.

Chapter 4, 'Introducing graphs', explains the purposes of graphs and gives recommendations for graph selection. Most of the chapter is dedicated to graph design.

Chapter 5, 'Using graphs', examines bar, line, and pie charts. It describes the advantages and disadvantages of each type and directions for their creation. It also looks at scattergrams, superimposed graphs, and pictographs.

Chapter 6, 'Table or graph?', sets out criteria for choosing between tables and graphs for your data.

Chapter 7, 'Communicating numbers', explains the necessity of knowing your audience, and recommends practices for using numbers both in text and in oral presentations.

Chapter 8, 'Using technology', discusses creating tables and graphs with common software and displaying information in print, on computer screens, and through presentation software.

Part B, the reference section, provides checklists, a glossary, resources, a case study, and exercises for further study.

Using this book

We do not anticipate that people will read this book from cover to cover. It is much more like a cookbook you can dip into when you wish. We suggest, however, that you might wish to begin by reading Chapter 2 on plain figures and Chapter 4, introducing graphs. These two chapters will give you a good grounding in using numbers to communicate.

This book contains many examples of tables, graphs, and language. For ease of reference good practice is indicated with a ✔.

2 | Handling numbers

Introduction

Many people find numbers a trial. One reason is that numbers are frequently presented in a muddled fashion without context or apparent organization. Making sense of these numbers and working out their relevance is time-consuming and discouraging. Presenting figures in a succinct and unequivocal manner makes them easier to comprehend. People are more likely to understand when something is concrete rather than abstract, for instance:

The numbers 7, 39, 1842 mean nothing by themselves. But it's rather interesting to learn that 'Minnie Hobbes had 7 children and 39 cousins when she died in 1842' or that 'only 39 of the 1,842 people were seriously injured in the boating accident and 7 of them are in intensive care'.

Numbers (or figures—the words are interchangeable) are most interesting when the presentation emphasizes their context. To make numeric information relevant and memorable, we need to select the correct data and present it in a way that emphasizes what is important.

Six principles on presenting numbers for easy communication are set out in this book, five of them in this chapter. They can help you organize figures, identify what is important about them, and decide how to communicate them to your audience. More than anything else they bring out the patterns and exceptions in the numbers. By following these simple rules, numeric lists and tables become coherent, interesting, and memorable.

The six rules of plain figures:

1 Put figures in an order.

2 Add focus to figures.

These rules were first set out by Professor A .S. C. Ehrenberg of the London Business School in the 1970s.

3 Keep comparisons close.

4 Round figures for clarity.

5 Provide a summary.

6 Use layout to guide the eyes.

Information on layout appears in Chapter 4. The other rules of plain figures are discussed here.

1 Put figures in an order

List numbers in a logical order; most often this will be largest to smallest.

Size order helps the reader make comparisons, revealing patterns and exceptions. Patterns are likely to tell us something important ('Sales rose consistently'). Exceptions raise important questions (why did sales rise everywhere but Ireland?).

By listing numbers from largest to smallest, readers are able to subtract the figures in their heads. Putting numbers in size order allows readers to make comparisons quickly.

Most people find it easier to subtract

$$878$$
$$-152$$

than to subtract

$$152$$
$$-878$$

Example 2.1 Order figures numerically

✔

US household penetration of consumer electronics		US household penetration of consumer electronics	
	%		%
Camcorder	39	Colour TV	98
Car CD player	31	VCR deck	94
Colour TV	98	Cordless phone	81
Cordless phone	81	Wireless phone	66
Direct-to-home satellite	17	Personal computer	60
DVD player	25	Home CD player	57
Home CD player	57	Camcorder	39
Home theatre system	25	Car CD player	31
Personal computer	60	DVD player	25
VCR deck	94	Home theatre system	25
Wireless phone	66	Direct-to-home satellite	17

Source: Consumer Electronics Association Annual Report, 2002

The alphabetical order, on the left, is confusing compared to the size order. In the list to the right the popularity of television stands out against the rarity of the direct-to-home satellite. Size order lets readers see the relative standing of each item.

Large amounts of data

Order becomes critical with long lists and tables. Size order guides the reader through the numbers, making the relationships clearer.

In the first table below, alphabetical order produces a random array of numbers, which are difficult to compare.

In the second table both rows and columns are now ordered by size. The reader can quickly spot the relative sales of each product and in each region.

The revised arrangement helps readers spot three notable factors. Orange outsells all other products, accounting for double the sales of Blue. A second pattern is that sales in the

Example 2.2 Ordering large amounts of data

Sales, 2002, by territory

	East	North	South	West
Blue	360	410	380	420
Green	300	330	340	470
Orange	800	830	820	840
Red	210	230	200	240
Yellow	360	390	380	390

Sales, 2002, by territory

	West	North	South	East
Orange	840	830	820	800
Blue	420	410	380	360
Yellow	390	390	380	360
Green	470	330	340	300
Red	240	230	200	210

east are consistently lower, regardless of product. Finally there
is an exception in the west, where Green sales are much larger
than in other regions. These patterns are visible with numeric
order.

If you could not spot these three factors, don't despair. That is
why we need to add focus to the presentation.

Exceptions

- In some cases alphabetical, chronological, or another
  natural order will be right. Consider how readers will
  use the information. Organize the data so that the
  arrangement serves their purpose.

- In a series of tables, order should be consistent.

2 Add focus to figures

You can help readers understand what your numbers mean by listing averages, totals, and percentages, which helps focus attention on the message embodied in the numbers.

- Averages provide a row or column summary. They help to bring out the patterns and exceptions in the data.

- Totals give readers the big picture.

- Percentages give an idea of proportion.

Help readers to make their own deductions.

Averages

Generally you should choose among averages, totals, or percentages. Presenting all three, or two of the three, can clutter a table, making it difficult to see its overall message.

Example 2.3 Averages give focus

In the table below, row averages are added to Example 2.2.

✔

Sales, 2002, by territory

	West	North	South	East	Average
Orange	840	830	820	800	823
Blue	420	410	380	360	393
Yellow	390	390	380	360	380
Green	470	330	340	300	360
Red	240	230	200	210	220

There is a gap between the regions columns and that of the averages. This extra space helps readers distinguish the different type of data being presented.

The patterns and exceptions are now even easier to see. The poor sales in the east can be identified by comparison with the average (800 compared to 823, 360 compared to 393, etc.). The exceptional sales of Green in the west are also obvious (470 to an average of 360). It is apparent that the average sales of Orange are double those of other colours.

Totals

Totals and percentages are additional tools for focusing. Though common, totals are not always necessary. Averages frequently provide better comparisons. However, there is nothing misleading about totals. Include totals when you think your audience will need them, for instance in budgets.

Numbers give an idea of volume; percentages an idea of proportion.

Example 2.4 Totals help give the big picture

✔

Sales, 2002, by territory

	West	North	South	East	Total
Orange	840	830	820	800	3,290
Blue	420	410	380	360	1,570
Yellow	390	390	380	360	1,520
Green	470	330	340	300	1,440
Red	240	230	200	210	880
Total	2,360	2,190	2,120	2,030	

Percentages

Percentages are rarely as helpful as averages, but do show proportions.

Example 2.5 Percentages show proportions

See Chapter 3 on creating simple tables.

The first table shows a poor use of percentages. The numbers and percentages intersect, making it impossible for the eye to scan across a row and to make comparisons with ease.

Sales, 2002, number and percentage by territory

	West	%	North	%	South	%	East	%	Total
Orange	840	36	830	38	820	39	800	39	3,290
Blue	420	18	410	19	380	18	360	18	1,570
Yellow	390	17	390	18	380	18	360	18	1,520
Green	470	20	330	15	340	16	300	15	1,440
Red	240	10	230	11	200	9	210	10	880
Totals	2,360	100	2,190	100	2,120	100	2,030	100	

Percentages have been rounded so sums may not total.

If your readers need both the numbers and the proportions, give them two simple tables rather than one complex one.

✔

Sales, 2002, by territory

	West	North	South	East	Total
Orange	840	830	820	800	3,290
Blue	420	410	380	360	1,570
Yellow	390	390	380	360	1,520
Green	470	330	340	300	1,440
Red	240	230	200	210	880
Total	2,360	2,190	2,120	2,030	9,120

✔

Percentage sales, 2002, by territory

	West	North	South	East
Orange	36	38	39	39
Blue	18	19	18	18
Yellow	17	18	18	18
Green	20	15	16	15
Red	10	11	9	10
Total	100	100	100	100

Figures have been rounded so sums may not total.

3 Keep comparisons close

Numbers to be compared should be physically close to one another. This proximity helps your readers compare the numbers.

Figures in columns are physically closer to one another than figures in rows. Rows are necessarily separated by blank space. Numbers in columns are easy to add, subtract, and compare. We don't normally encounter numbers horizontally, so the unfamiliar layout adds to the difficulty. Therefore, when designing a table you should put numbers to be compared in columns, not rows.

Example 2.6   Compare in columns

Winnipeg	Edmonton	Saskatoon	Calgary	Regina
788,000	776,000	764,000	731,000	710,000

✔

Winnipeg	788,000
Edmonton	776,000
Saskatoon	764,000
Calgary	731,000
Regina	710,000

The first list, organized in a long row, demands reading across blank space. In a single-spaced column, the numbers are physically close to each other. The figures in the second presentation are easier to add, subtract, and compare.

Compared to what?

We can only keep comparisons close if we know which items to compare. Which comparisons will be most beneficial to your readers? What are they interested in?

Example 2.7 Selecting comparisons

The table below shows exports of apples and pears over several years. The first presentation emphasizes comparison between apples and pears.

Tonnes of fruit exported 1990–1999

	1990	1993	1996	1999
Apples	54,000	53,000	58,000	62,000
Pears	4,300	4,440	4,600	4,800

✔

Tonnes of fruit exported 1990–1999

	Apples	Pears
1990	54,000	4,300
1993	53,000	4,400
1996	58,000	4,600
1999	62,000	4,800

How can you know what your audience needs? Try showing your work to representatives of the groups you will address. At least show it to a colleague. The professional term for this practice is **usability testing**.

The reorganized table highlights the changes of each product over the years. Given that exports of apples are disproportionate to that of pears, it is unlikely that many people would want to compare the two. Most readers would be interested in tracking how each product increased over the years.

Compare like with like

You can only compare numbers that are similar. Figures come in various forms—measuring miles and kilometres, counting armies, navies, weapons, and money, comparing males and females. It's up to you to transform these numbers into useful information: distance, costs of military units, and spending patterns of males and females.

Example 2.8 Compare like with like

Chilled meats	Calories		Chilled meats	Calories per 4oz/100g
Beef (4oz/100g)	225		Salami	500
Chicken (4oz/100g)	153		Liver sausage	300
Ham (4oz/100g)	109		Beef	225
Liver sausage (1oz/25g)	75		Chicken	153
Salami (1oz/25g)	125		Ham	109

Source: *Woman's Own Diet Special,1998*

This first list, reprinted from a magazine, uses two types of measurements—ounces and grams—hidden in brackets. Many readers would conclude that liver sausage and salami have fewer calories than beef and chicken.

The revised version uses a single scale (4oz/100g) throughout, making the numbers comparative. A single scale maintains accuracy. While it takes more effort to calculate items on the same basis, it does have the advantage of clarity.

The error would probably have been prevented if the writers had systematically reordered their numbers by size.

4 Round figures for clarity

Rounding is a simple technique that improves communication dramatically. It makes numbers easier to understand, remember and use.

Remembering

Take a number like 249,687: people can remember a detailed number if they are not interrupted. They can remember the rounded version (250,000) even after interruptions. Detailed numbers are difficult to recall because of limitations in our short-term memory. Rounded numbers are memorable.

Mental arithmetic

Most people can perform mental arithmetic with numbers of two digits, but not with more detailed figures. For instance, try to compare 723 and 238 without pen and paper. When they are rounded to 720 and 240, it is easy to see that the first is three times the second. Rounding makes mental arithmetic easier.

Example 2.9 The benefits of rounding

Consider this short table:

Round:
(a number)
altered for
convenience of
expression or
calculation…

New Oxford Dictionary of English

Evidence supporting the advantages of rounded numbers goes back to the 1920s.

Sales of pencils, thousands				
	1996	1998	2000	2002
UK	256.8	459.3	495.7	498.8
Canada	73.3	89.4	87.9	98.8
Total	330.1	548.7	583.6	597.6

Can we remember any of the numbers if we look away? What can we say about the sales without looking back at the table?

Understanding a set of numbers involves comparing them. This isn't easy with the above table. Mentally comparing the total pencils sold in 1996 and 2002 is difficult (597.6 minus 330.1 equals 267.5). Most of us consciously or unconsciously round numbers first.

When we present the same data rounded, readers find it much easier to make comparisons and remember the numbers:

✔

Sales of pencils, thousands				
	1996	1998	2000	2002
UK	260	460	500	500
Canada	73	89	88	99
Total	330	550	590	600

Figures have been rounded so sums may not total.

Using the rounded figures we can quickly see that total pencil sales nearly doubled between 1996 and 2002. (Most of us can mentally calculate 600 minus 330, equalling 270.) We can also see that almost twice as many pencils were sold in the UK in 2002 as in 1996 (500,000 against 260,000). Further, it is clear that in Canada the difference in sales was much less.

Most people will be able to recall these patterns later: sales in 2002 were twice those of 1996, except in Canada.

Making decisions

Most decisions in management and elsewhere are made on rounded figures; details of more than two digits rarely influence a decision. If you are buying a car, do you think to yourself 'I have £7,224.16'? Or do you think, 'I have £7,200'? We round all the time to simplify and compare.

Accuracy

Some people resist rounded numbers, arguing that they are not accurate. 'Accurate' figures often do not exist. The only figures available may be estimates or numbers captured at a certain time. For instance, the population of Canada was officially estimated at 31,592,805 in July 2001. But every day people are born and die, come and go. The precise population is not known and does not matter: the rounded number (32,000,000) serves almost all purposes.

Of course, auditors, precision engineers, and pharmacists cannot round their work. They need to account for every penny, every millimetre, and every dose. But most of us are not auditors, engineers, or pharmacists. And even they can round when their figures are for general management purposes and public communication.

Tip
What if some of your readers want the precise numbers? Go ahead and round the numbers for clarity, but include a list of sources for those interested.

Rounding to two digits

At school you were probably taught fixed rounding; all figures are converted to tens, hundreds, or thousands. An alternative method, called 'variable rounding', is statistically valid, simple to calculate, and more practical for everyday use. With variable rounding you round to two (occasionally three) effective digits, regardless of the size of the number.

Variable rounding has the advantage over fixed rounding in that it maintains all figures, and no number, no matter how small, is reduced to zero.

Example 2.10 Fixed and variable rounding

Exercises on rounding appear in Part B.

Fixed rounding (column B) reduces some items to nil. In variable rounding (column C) all the numbers are rounded to two digits.

A Original	B Fixed rounding to thousands	C Variable rounding to two effective digits
28,732	29,000	29,000
4,116	4,000	4,100
267	0	270
42	0	42

| Exceptions

When figures in a series are numerically close you need more than two digits. Showing only two digits is too approximate and will introduce unacceptable errors. For example, let us look at the series 857, 865, 877, and 889. Rounding to two digits would give us 860, 870, 880, and 890 and an effective loss of precision. When figures are numerically close, use three digits.

Rounding totals

You need to round totals independently from other numbers. Do this by adding up the original numbers and noting the total. Then round each individual number, including the total.

Without independent rounding, errors are likely to creep in. It is easy to mistakenly round twice. Don't round the figures; add them up and then round that total. Rounding twice introduces unacceptable mathematical errors.

Don't rely on the rounding function of your spreadsheet. Be sure to check that your program totals the actual, not the rounded, numbers.

People are also often tempted to fiddle the numbers, to make the columns add up. Though appealing, this practice distorts the numbers far more than any rounding does. Both precision (of the exact figures) and proportion (of rounding) are lost.

Example 2.11 Rounding totals

Sales of tools ($)	Original	Rounded
Ontario	8,488,723	8,500,000
British Columbia	6,308,452	6,300,000
Quebec	640,891	640,000
Newfoundland	481,438	480,000
Total	15,919,504	16,000,000

Figures have been rounded so sums may not total.

The total in the third column has been rounded 'independently' and, as frequently happens, this figure does not equal the sum of the rounded figures above (which come to

15,920,000). Users will sometimes notice the disparity; a short explanation is helpful. Add a line at the end to your table saying, something like: 'Figures have been rounded independently, so columns may not equal totals.' Another alternative is to omit the total and add a sentence at the bottom of the numbers stating: 'The total expenditure was approximately $16 million for the period.'

5 Provide a summary

Include a succinct written summary in the text.

Summaries give you the opportunity of pointing out any patterns or exceptions in the figures. They let you explain why you think the data is worthy of attention. It is a second opportunity to get your message across.

Use your text (or speech) to emphasize conclusions, trends, anomalies, and patterns.

Good news!
Writing a summary helps you think clearly about what the figures indicate and the purpose of including them.

Tips

- Always include a table or graph with an explanation in your text or speech. If you don't tell the readers what the numbers mean, many of them will never know.

- Writing 'Table X shows that there has been little change over the last five years' is more helpful to readers than merely stating 'Please see Table X for the outcomes.'

- Summarize the overall point or message of the table. There is no need to mention most numbers.

Example 2.12 Written summary

The table in Example 2.3 (reprinted below) contains twenty-five numbers. Readers will need direction to work out the meaning and important features. The summary we give is written for a general audience.

Table A: Sales, 2002, by territory

	West	North	South	East	Average
Orange	840	830	820	800	823
Blue	420	410	380	360	393
Yellow	390	390	380	360	380
Green	470	330	340	300	360
Red	240	230	200	210	220

Sales (see Table A) are closely spread across the four territories, although sales in the west are higher then other areas and substantially higher than the east. Sales of Orange are twice as high as any other item and sales of Green are disproportionately high in the west.

This direct statement, explains both what the table does (sales across the divisions) and the specific features of the figures. By citing a reference number you ensure that readers consult the correct table.

To sum up . . .

This chapter explains five of the six rules of plain figures. These rules will help organize numbers so they can be understood quickly and communicated effectively.

The rules are:

1 Put figures in an order. Order helps readers see the relationship between numbers. Size order is usually appropriate.

2 Add focus. Averages give a point for comparison, helping readers to discern patterns and exceptions in the data. Totals give the big picture. Percentages, though less critical, are useful for establishing proportion.

3 Keep comparisons close. Physical proximity helps comparisons. Figures in columns are easier to compare than

those in rows. In order to use this principle, you must choose what numbers should be compared and ensure the items are comparable.

4 Round numbers to improve communication. Rounding is an easy measure that simplifies numbers. As a general rule, use variable rounding to two digits.

5 Provide a summary in the text. Help your reader understand the data and connect it to your overall argument or point.

These guidelines are easily incorporated into almost anyone's work. By following them, you can improve your presentation of numbers and hence help your audience to understand your point. Some will even be grateful for the clear display.

3 | Using tables

Learning to design a
readable table is like
learning to ride a
bike—it takes trial and
error.

Tables list numbers in a systematic fashion. Tables supplement, simplify, explain, and condense written material. Their design should be based on convenience to the reader.

Well-designed tables are easily understood: patterns and exceptions stand out, at least once they have been explained. Tables are underestimated and underused. This is mainly because of poor layout, which confuses rather than clarifies the data. Tables are more flexible than graphs and, when well designed, are as memorable.

You can use tables to:

- show a multitude of figures (in some cases hundreds);

- show a wide range of figures (for instance the population of every town in Ontario);

- list precise numbers;

- extract numbers easily;

- identify patterns and exceptions in the data.

There are two types of table:

- demonstration tables, which organize selected figures to show a particular point. Most tables used in reports, at meetings, and in publications are demonstration tables.

- reference tables, which provide exact and comprehensive information. Train schedules, sports scores, and stock market listings are all reference tables.

These will be explained later in the chapter. First we go through some general points.

Components of a table

Below we set out the different components of a table.

Example 3.1 Components of a table

✔

Number and title

Column headings

Row headings

Multi-column heading

Table 3.1 GP and diabetic services, 2000

Towns	GP practices		
	Number	Number providing diabetic services	% providing diabetic services
Laindon	40	38	95
Wakeford	29	27	93
Rosemont*	29	25	86
Northlands	34	29	85
Port Royal	36	30	83
Flanshaw	62	32	52
Total	230	181	82

Source

Footnote

Source: Health Authority Annual Report, 2001

* Including Northview and Douglas.

Patterns and exceptions

In the best tables, patterns and exceptions stand out, at least once they have been explained. In Table 3.1 above, most areas have between 29 and 40 GPs and over 80 per cent of those provided a diabetic service. The exception is Flanshaw, where there are over 60 GPs but only 52 per cent of them have a diabetic service.

Patterns and exceptions indicate what is important about the data.

Successful tables

Successful tables communicate their purpose with ease. They are designed for efficient comprehension and easy use. They contain the minimum of numbers to serve their purpose.

When you are designing tables, keep in mind three principles:

- simplicity of layout;

- clarity of wording;

- attention to page design.

These are explained below.

Simplicity of layout

A simple and uncluttered table will communicate the numbers more successfully than a 'busy' or decorated one. Poor layout, rather than difficult material, accounts for most confusion with tables.

Grid lines

Grid lines clutter tables without adding information. Vertical lines stop the eyes scanning across a row of figures to make comparisons. Even before you put numbers in the grid, it is crowded with lines.

Consider this figure:

We recognize the lines as a triangle, even though the drawing is incomplete. Similarly, the eye does not need grid lines to

Look at suggestions in Chapter 8 on using technology for tips on how to create user-friendly tables and graphs.

Grids were necessary for creating handwritten tables, such as in ledger books. Computers, especially spreadsheet programs, make these obsolete.

follow the layout of a table. The arrangement of columns and rows create their own order for the reader.

Example 3.2 The Dreaded Grid

Grid lines dominate the first table below. The vertical lines stop the eye scanning across the row. The horizontal lines interrupt numeric comparisons and make subtraction more difficult.

Edward Tufte coined the term 'the Dreaded Grid' to describe these lines, which create muddles and introduce ugliness to tables, without adding information.

Table A Patients at general hospitals by department, 1999, thousands

	Wakeford	West Manchester	Chester University	Total
Outpatients	380	280	180	840
Community contacts	150	130	29	310
Accident & Emergency	110	80	59	250
Inpatients	45	54	35	130
Day cases	40	26	19	85
Total	730	570	320	1,600

Source: NHS Local Implementation Strategy, 2000
Figures have been rounded so sums may not total.

In the second table blank space divides the rows and columns. Notice that significant space is inserted between the column headings and totals.

✔

Table B Patients at general hospitals by department, 1999, thousands

	Wakeford	West Manchester	Chester University	Total
Outpatients	380	280	180	840
Community contacts	150	130	29	310
Accident & Emergency	110	80	59	50
Inpatients	45	54	35	130
Day cases	40	26	19	85
Total	730	570	320	1,600

Source: NHS Local Implementation Strategy, 2000
Figures have been rounded so sums may not total.

| **Layout tips**

■ Align numbers and column headings to the right. This establishes uniformity among different lengths of numbers, allowing you to use their natural shape to communicate. Spreadsheets tend to align headings to the left and numbers to the right, inviting confusion.

■ Single-spaced tables keep figures close to one another. In longer tables, a blank line inserted every four or five lines helps readers keep their place.

Clarity of wording

Incomplete and inaccurate wording can make an otherwise useful table incomprehensible. Wording consists of titles, column and row headings, and any other text on the table, for instance a source or a footnote. If the information contained in words is insufficient or confusing, many people will ignore your table altogether.

Table titles

Titles should be definitive and comprehensive, giving all the necessary information. Readers need to know:

What   The subject of the table: patients, staffing levels, home electronics, Canadian malls with restaurant facilities, etc. Detail may be included.

Where   Location: Manchester, South America, Laindon Community Centre, Dr Abdul's clinic, etc.

When   Dates or period covered: 2002, 1945–75, May and June, etc.

Units   What measurement are used: thousands, hundreds; barrels of oil, grams of fat, etc.

It is also helpful to give tables a reference number or letter. This allows you to cite its reference in your summary, reducing the chances of confusion.

Below are some examples of how titles can be set out on a table.

Example 3.3 Comprehensive titles

Reference number	Subject	Detail (optional)	Location	Dates or period covered	Units
Table 5.3	Unemployment	Males and females	Paisley	1992–2002	% of workforce
Table A	Patients at local general hospitals	By department	Manchester	1999	Thousands
Table 5a	Satisfaction levels	Local playgrounds	Newton Hill	May 2002	Numbers

Labelling columns and headings

The labels on columns and headings need to be coherent for your readers. We suggest:

■ Avoiding abbreviations, unless they are well known, for instance BBC or the UN. Abbreviations confuse and irritate people unfamiliar with them.

■ Eliminating footnotes, which are disruptive. Try to include all necessary information in your headings. If you do need footnotes (and academic papers often require them), mark them with asterisks rather than footnote numbers. Surprisingly, some readers confuse footnote numbers with the contents of the table.

■ Including sources on all tables. This not only helps the reader but is beneficial when you want to check the information in eighteen months' time.

Does GM mean grams, General Motors, genetically modified, general manager, a grant-maintained school, the George Medal, or a chess grand master?

Style

By using upper and lower case text rather than all CAPITALS, you make the words easier to read. People tend to read by the shape of words, and capital letters have less shape.

Make sure your text is large enough to read. There is some evidence that tables are easier to read if slightly smaller than the rest of the text. Be aware of your audience, however. If your document is for the public, then 12-point type is recommended. Many people over fifty find smaller-size print significantly difficult to read.

Keep headings succinct

Succinct column headings help organize the information. The table title should be comprehensive; let it carry the information.

Example 3.4 Shortening column headings

One method of shortening headings is by transferring some information into the title. This was done in Table 3.2 above. Here is the original:

Patients, 1999, thousands			
	Wakeford Healthcare NHS Trust	West Manchester Hospital NHS Trust	Chester University NHS Trust
Outpatients Department			
Community contacts			
Accident & Emergency Department			
Inpatients Department			
Day cases			

The final version added 'at general hospitals' and 'by department' to the title. Repetitious and unnecessary information, such as 'NHS Trusts' and 'Departments' can be deleted.

Patients at general hospitals by department, 1999, thousands

	Wakeford	West Manchester	Chester University
Outpatients			
Community contacts			
Accident & Emergency			
Inpatients			
Day cases			

Attention to page design

Your tables and explanatory text should complement one another. Tables need to be close to their explanation, preferably on the same page. Turning pages prevents the reader from moving efficiently between text and the numbers.

Tables look best either centred on the page or aligned to the left. For best effect, place them at the top or the bottom of a page. The alternative—surrounding a table with text—makes reading both the text and the table more difficult.

Whatever placement you choose, stick with it throughout the document. Readers can then find tables easily and the document will look professional.

To improve page design you can:

■ apply the principles of plain figures to organize your numbers;

■ refer to your tables in your text. Don't leave your table unidentified, unexplained and alone;

■ ensure tables are only as wide as the data demands (see Example 3.1). When tables are artificially stretched across the page, the numbers are harder to compare. For easy communication, keep comparisons close.

| # Demonstration tables

Demonstration tables make a point or an argument. They should be short and to the point. Include only the numbers needed to explain the message.

A good demonstration table is easy to read and understand. Patterns and exceptions stand out, at least once they have been explained in the summary. If readers have problems understanding your table, they are unlikely to use the data.

A 'less is more' approach is necessary. Most often several short tables will successfully communicate better than a single complex table. Too much data becomes incomprehensible; it intimidates the audience, who are counting on you for information, not a muddle.

Example 3.5 Three smaller tables replace one complex table

The following table is crowded and confusing.

Remember that any series of tables must be consistent in layout, style, and order.

Table 3.5 Restaurant facilities, Canadian malls, 2002: number of facilities

	Standard malls			Premier malls			Grand total
	With restaurant	With food court	Total	With restaurant	With food court	Total	
Montreal	25	31	56	11	8	19	75
Vancouver	22	6	38	12	6	18	56
Toronto	16	12	28	7	8	15	43
Halifax	14	11	25	3	3	6	31
Saskatoon	4	3	7	4	1	5	12
Totals	81	63	154	37	26	63	217

By using three simple tables, as below, you can present the same numbers more clearly. Each table focuses on one aspect of the data. Notice that each of these tables has only eighteen numbers, as opposed to the forty-two figures in the comprehensive table.

Table 3.5a Restaurant facilities in standard malls, January 2002, Canada

	With restaurants	With food court	Total
Montreal	25	31	56
Vancouver	22	16	38
Toronto	16	12	28
Halifax	14	11	25
Saskatoon	4	3	7
Totals	81	73	154

Table 3.5b Restaurant facilities in premier malls, January 2002, Canada

	With restaurants	With food court	Total
Montreal	11	8	19
Vancouver	12	6	18
Toronto	7	8	15
Halifax	3	3	6
Saskatoon	4	1	5
Totals	37	26	63

Table 3.5c Restaurant facilities in all malls, January 2002, Canada

	With restaurants	With food court	Total
Montreal	36	39	75
Vancouver	34	22	56
Toronto	23	20	43
Halifax	17	14	31
Saskatoon	8	4	12
Totals	118	99	217

Reference tables

Reference tables (also called 'look-up tables') are used for specific information, such as train schedules, sports scores, and financial records. Unlike a demonstration table, a reference table does not argue a point. Its purpose is to be there when people need the information.

Reference tables by their nature contain large amounts of information. They can be made readable chiefly by adopting the techniques discussed earlier in this chapter.

A few tips may help you:

■ Use detailed numbers. Numbers are not usually rounded in reference tables. You don't want to miss the 1.37 train because the time was rounded to 1.40.

■ Reference tables are usually found in appendices to reports. Rarely do they appear in a report itself.

■ In longer tables, use a blank space rather than commas to separate thousands (For example, 380 000 rather than 380,000). This reduces clutter.

■ Insert blank space. In longer tables insert a blank row every four or five lines. This helps the reader to identify rows and hold their place.

Example 3.6 A government reference table

This excerpt is part of an official government reference table. Well-designed tables like this show that a large quantity of readable information (this has nearly ninety numbers) can be put on a single page. Note the footnotes and the enquiry phone number on the bottom right.

Table 12a Public transport usage in metropolitan areas, millions

	West Midlands	Greater Manchester	Merseyside	South Yorkshire	West Yorkshire	Tyne & Wear	Greater London
Bus passenger journeys							
1991/92	389	260	191	177	240	220	1,149
1992/93	356	252	178	176	231	189	1,129
1993/94	355	236	166	166	232	182	1,117
1994/95	381	226	168	163	222	170	1,167
1995/96	358	224	165	158	210	168	1,205
1996/97	349	212	163	150	207	165	1,242
1997/98	368	211	153	144	200	161	1,294
1998/99	353	217	150	135	186	154	1,279
Rail passenger kilometres[1]							
1991/92	—	241[2]	325	—	269	318[3]	5,927[4]
1992/93	—	269[2]	312	—	287	312[3]	5,791[4]
1993/94	—	295[2]	306	—	299	312[3]	5,853[4]
1994/95	—	276[2]	298	44	226	306[3]	6,106[4]
1995/96	—	293[2]	288	45	254	300[3]	6,407[4]
1996/97	—	301[2]	313	47	265	293[3]	6,239[4]
1997/98	—	303[2,5]	310	47	293	288[3]	6,582[4]
1998/99	—	314[2,5]	336	47	304	277[3]	6,860[4]

1 Rail services in metropolitan areas are metro systems and those supported under Section 20 of the 1968 Transport Act.
2 From 1992/93, includes estimated figures for Metrolink.
3 Includes Tyne & Wear Metro.
4 London Underground and Docklands Light Railway only.
5 Estimate.

Enquiries: 020-7890-3098 (Department of the Environment, Transport and the Regions)
http://www.transtat.dft.gov.uk/tables/2000/tsma/tsma.htm)
© Crown copyright—used with permission

To sum up . . .

Tables are an excellent device for displaying large quantities and a wide range of figures. Demonstration tables present selected figures to make a point, showing a trend or suggesting a cause. Reference tables use exact numbers to list specific data.

Successful tables communicate with ease. Patterns and exceptions stand out, at least once you have explained them in your summary. The best tables organize contents for the reader's convenience through simplicity of layout, clarity of wording, and attention to page design.

Tables need comprehensive titles and succinct headings. The layout should be simple, replacing grid lines with white space. Consistency in alignment, close proximity of numbers, and page placement contribute to effective tables. Several short, simple tables are likely to communicate more easily than one complex table.

4 Introducing graphs

Introduction

A graph is a diagram showing numerical trends and relationships. A good graph makes information vivid, memorable, and meaningful. The best graphs communicate their purpose with ease.

This book covers a variety of graphs: bar, line, pie, pictographs, scattergrams, and superimposed graphs. Each individual type is discussed in the next chapter.

Graphs excel at demonstrating patterns and relationships that are difficult to see in tables or to describe in words. They are best at showing a specific message rather than a general one; better at displaying large differences than fine detail. They are less versatile than tables, but surpass tables for dramatic effect.

Example 4.1 Good graphs communicate simply

The best graphs—the ones that communicate with ease—are both memorable and simple. Although this line graph contains nearly 60 data points, the design makes it simple to understand.

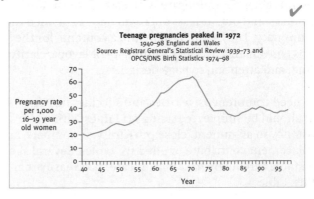

Looking and telling

There are two reasons for using graphs, that is, when you are:

Looking to discover

Graphs help solve the puzzle of the numbers. When examining unfamiliar data, you can try out several different graphs to identify trends, relationships, and other meanings. The outcome of the discovery stage should be a clear understanding of what the numbers mean.

Telling a story

Once you have settled on your message, design your graph to tell the story. At this stage the graph should no longer be a puzzle but have a specific message.

When using graphs for discovery, you are free to try any approach consistent with the nature of the data. When drawing up a graph for a report or presentation, the advice and suggestions in this chapter should be useful.

See Chapter 6 when choosing between a table or graph.

Successful graphs communicate with ease. The best graphs will

■ show trends and relationships;

■ attract attention;

■ improve on the data being shown in a table or in text.

Creating graphs

Graphs benefit from four features:

1 clarity of message;

2 simplicity of design;

3 clarity of words;

4 integrity of intentions and action.

1 Clarity of message

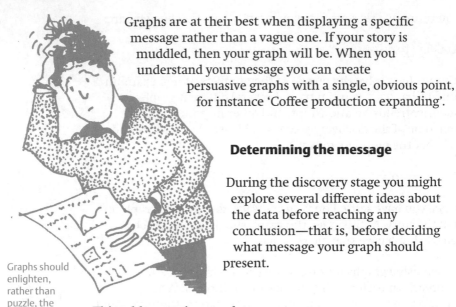

Graphs are at their best when displaying a specific message rather than a vague one. If your story is muddled, then your graph will be. When you understand your message you can create persuasive graphs with a single, obvious point, for instance 'Coffee production expanding'.

Determining the message

During the discovery stage you might explore several different ideas about the data before reaching any conclusion—that is, before deciding what message your graph should present.

Graphs should enlighten, rather than puzzle, the reader.

This table contains raw data:

Sales of cars 1996–2002

	Models			
	A	B	C	D
1996	33,000	44,000	49,000	25,000
1997	35,000	38,000	47,000	22,000
1998	40,000	40,000	42,000	21,000
1999	41,000	44,000	37,000	23,000
2000	45,000	44,000	34,000	24,000
2001	47,000	41,000	30,000	24,000
2002	51,000	42,000	25,000	23,000

You might wish to emphasise Model A, with the message: 'Sales of Model A increase steadily.' Alternatively, you could compare sales, in which case your message might be 'Sales of Model A swell as Model C slumps.' Or you might wish to isolate 2002 sales, directing the reader through the message, 'Model A sales are double sales for Models C and D.'

Once you have decided on what you want to say, you can choose which type of graph to use—say a line chart or a bar graph.

You can also use your message as the title of the graph.

The title

Good titles direct the reader to what is important. Often graph titles explain what the subject is, but they do not tell the reader the message.

Make your graph titles active and informative

Replace generalities with specifics and action words.

% Sales by region for 2002	Sales slump in north-east
House prices by quarter	House prices escalate
Canadian oil imports	Tumultuous oil imports in Canada
Number of staff by age and gender	Older males dominate senior ranks, but females challenge middle management

Titles on the left describe graphs, but ignore their innate drama. Titles can be either brief and snappy ('Car sales up!') or a longer phrase ('Profits down for the third quarter.'). What is important is that they tell the reader the point.

> Use the title to explain what is important about the graph.

Actions verbs (*slump*, *dominate*, and *challenge*) and adjectives (*tumultuous*) make titles still more attention-grabbing.

Helpful words

These words are useful to describe the action in graphs:

Rise: increase, climb, soar, mount, ascend, grow, escalate, upsurge, advance, boost, swell, multiply.

Fall: drop, tumble, plunge, plummet, reduce, descend, collapse, decline, fall, sink, dive.

Example 4.2 Titles focus the message

We know this graph is about company investments, but we aren't told what is important about them.

The Economist publishes professional-looking graphs each week, all of which have short titles that emphasize the point being made.

Most readers would probably conclude that the important story is that 'UK equities account for most of our investments'. But you might want to stress that property accounts for only 3 per cent of investments. You can draw the reader's attention through an alternative title, such as 'Property investment lags'.

2 Simplicity of design

Graphs rely on straightforward presentation. The sign of a good graph is that the message—the information—is emphasized, not the decoration.

Choosing a graph

To achieve design simplicity, choose one of the plainest graphs offered by your software. Microsoft Excel, for example, supplies over seventy choices of 'standard' graphs; only four or five of these are simple enough to communicate with ease. The most effective graphs are straightforward line, bar, and column charts.

Chart junk

Chart junk is decoration that interferes with meaning. Chart junk can be alluring to the beginner, but it clouds the message and looks amateurish.

Chart junk consists of unnecessary and distracting elements. The most common of these are grid lines, patterned bars and slices, backgrounds, borders, inappropriate and confusing colours, actual numbers and values. It includes any adornment that doesn't add information. Edward R. Tufte, who coined the term 'chart junk,' discusses many examples in detail in his books.

The following examples illustrate how clutter and inappropriate elements interfere with a graph's meaning.

Example 4.3 Varieties of chart junk

The first graph below is superior to the others because of its direct expression and lack of decoration. The labelling is clear and readable. Overall the emphasis is on what the data means (how the bars compare), not the design. The relationships between the bars are distinct and the graph makes a visual impact.

The Bauhaus saying 'Less is more' applies to graphs as well as art and architecture.

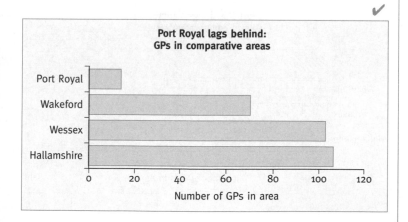

Grids. In the graph below, grids break up the space and interfere with the eye scanning the information. Remember, graphs should show broad trends and relationships, not fine detail.

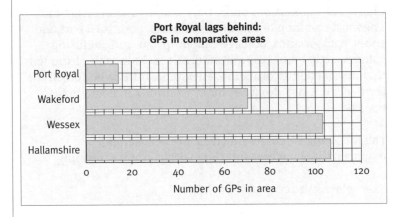

Patterns. Patterned bars confuse and distract from the message. They are unnecessary even in large graphs. Use plain white, greys, or blacks for fills.

Perfection is achieved not when there is nothing more to add, but when there is nothing left to take away.

Antoine de Saint-Exupéry

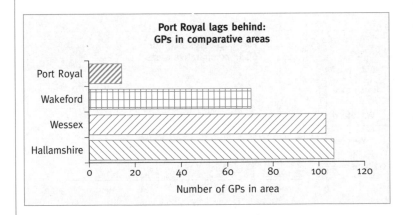

Background. Like all parts of the graph, backgrounds need to be kept unadorned. Patterned backgrounds disorient.

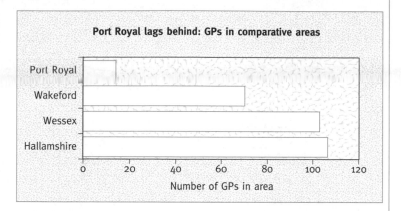

Border. Borders and shading likewise distract from the graph's information. Though legible, this graph takes longer to understand than does the simpler version.

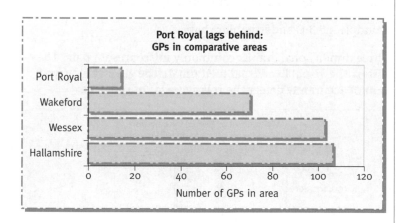

Values

Graphs communicate visually, not numerically. You can understand the message of the graph below without the numbers. Graphs excel when they are showing broad trends rather than detail.

Example 4.4 Values on graphs are redundant

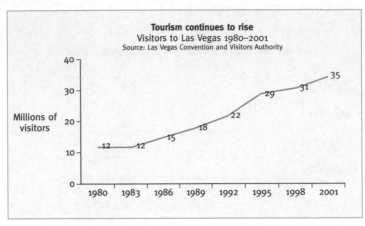

Shape

Avoid three-dimensional and odd-shaped graphs, which draw attention to the design rather than the content.

Example 4.5 3-D and irregular shapes

Three-dimensional graphs commonly misrepresent data. They distort the visual in a visual medium. In the graph below you cannot accurately detect the relative sizes of the bars.

Using colour?
See Chapter 8 for
advice.

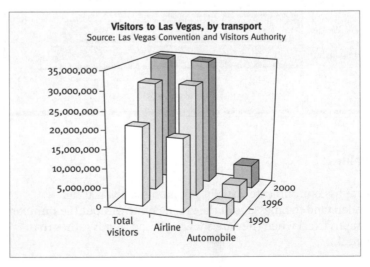

Odd shapes will not help readers understand your message or the data. Even readers who take the time to study the following graph are unlikely to make sense of it.

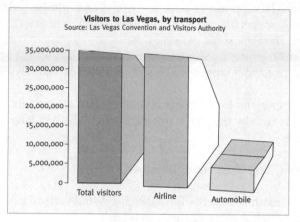

Visitors to Las Vegas, by transport
Source: Las Vegas Convention and Visitors Authority

Placing the graph on the page

The location of a graph within the document and on the page can add to its success in reaching readers. To achieve the greatest effects keep the following in mind:

■ Arrange any graph as close as possible to the text that explains or summarizes it. The best practice is to insert the graph immediately following the relevant paragraph. Graphs should not be in an appendix, where people can only find them with effort.

■ Align graphs to the left, or centre them on the page.

■ Place graphs at the top or bottom of the page. Avoid the middle, and never surround the graph with text.

Graphs look professional and communicate well when they are small. We suggest a maximum size of one-third of the screen or page size.

3 Clarity of words

Words that introduce, explain, and summarize help a graph communicate. Succinct wording also helps.

| # Lucid labels

Labels play an indispensable role in making graphs intelligible. The term 'label' refers to both the words and numbers. Advice on labelling specific types of graphs is found in the next chapter. Here are some general tips:

- Adopt succinct language. This takes practice, but pays off.

- Use upper and lower case text rather than all capitals. People read by the shape of words and CAPITALS have little shape.

- Employ text large enough to read.

- Place text horizontally for legibility. Avoid vertical or angled text, which is more difficult to read.

- Directly label each line, bar, and pie slice. The eye movements involved in flicking from the key legend to the graph interrupt memory. Direct labels are more convenient for the reader and reduce the risk of misinterpretation.

- Avoid abbreviations, unless well known, such as BBC or UN. Even within your own organization or profession you should think carefully before using abbreviations.

Example 4.6 Problems with labelling

This graph was designed for an annual report. Obscure abbreviations will put off many readers.

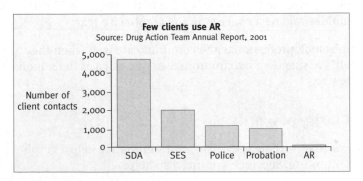

The second graph replaces abbreviations with long titles, which cannot fit underneath the bars. The key legend adds a distracting step for readers. If the bars and key are colour-coded, distinctions will be lost with photocopying.

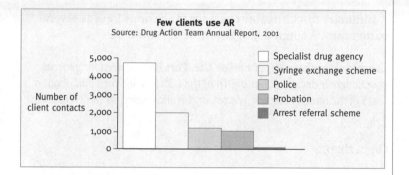

The final version is legible and lucid. Switching from columns to bars gives space to individual labelling of agency names on each bar.

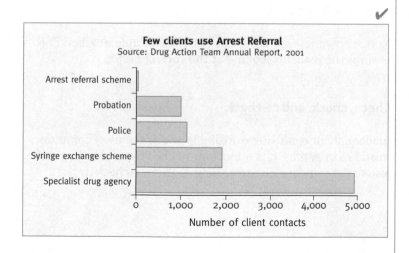

Include a summary or discussion

Graphs need to be discussed in your text. Never include an illustration without a summary or explanation. If the information in the graph does not merit discussion in the text, why include it at all?

Don't leave your graphs lonely and unexplained on a page.

A summary can be as short as a sentence or as long as several paragraphs. A summary of Example 4.3 could be:

Compared to other cities of similar size, Port Royal's need for general practioners is drastic. It has a fifth of the GPs in Wakeford and about a tenth of the number serving Wessex and Hallamshire, as shown in Figure 4.3.

Or, perhaps:

Example 4.3 shows the unequal distribution of general practitioners through out the county.

A summary of 4.6 might read:

Despite optimistic predictions, the Arrest Referral Scheme is underused, as shown in Example 4.6.

Notice how these explanations cite the example number. This ensures the reader is looking at the correct graph.

Check, check, and re-check

Inadequate or confusing wording is one of the most common mistakes in graphs. It is important to check your wording and also to get someone else to review it. Then re-check it.

4 Integrity of intentions and action

Many people think graphs and statistics lie and mislead the innocent. Ill-designed graphs leave users feeling disconcerted and excluded. Even well-educated readers can lack confidence in their ability to decipher graphs although most graphs require only simple arithmetic. Some graphs may be designed to mislead, but negligence is more frequently the cause of problem graphs.

Integrity is important in graphics, as in life. Your graphs need not only to be honest, but also to appear to be honest. Integrity in the presentation of information is more than following a few rules, although this always helps. You can avoid ambiguous graphs by double-checking the data and the presentation. It takes a commitment to want to communicate your figures openly and honestly. Here are a few suggestions.

Name your source

Attributing the source for the data—usually in smaller print at the bottom of your graph—gives it authority. It also saves people asking you where the numbers came from. In eighteen months' time, even you may not recall their origin. A list of sources or bibliography is good practice even if the public never sees your work. When your work is for public consumption, such openness is essential.

Scale

Choose scale carefully. It is the unit of comparison, and errors will mislead or confuse readers. Scale should accurately represent data and never obscure it.

The *British Standard Presentation of Tables and Charts* recommends that the scale should begin at zero, or that you should explain why it does not. This is to prevent misinterpretation.

Example 4.7 Scale represents data

Modifying the scale will change a graph's message. Below, three graphs present the same data. In the first graph, the vertical measurement (also known as the y-axis) starts at 1,500. The graph shows a dramatic decline from 1,750.

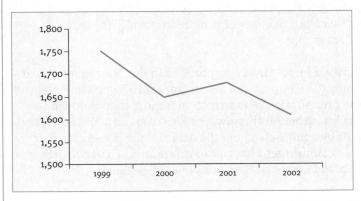

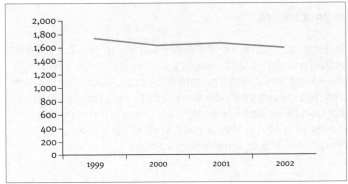

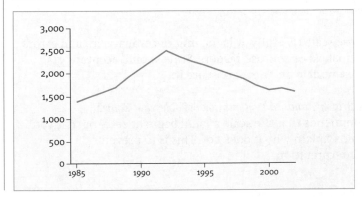

The first graph above is adequate if your job is to examine the four-year time spread. (If, for example, your report is about a policy change instituted in 1998.) You are likely to mislead readers if you claim to be discussing the larger picture. If there is a reason for starting the scale at 1,500, then state it.

The second graph starts in the same year, but at zero rather than 1,500. By starting the y-axis at zero we can see that the decline that appeared massive in the first graph is relatively slight.

The third version shows the long-term picture—it starts at 0 on the y-axis and in 1985. We can see now that the recent decline follows a long period of expansion.

The third graph might be fair, depending on the relevance of the long-term history. If in 2003 you are considering buying shares in the Hudson's Bay Company (founded in 1670), you do not need a 300-year share value history. Data for the last fifteen years would be appropriate.

Technical integrity

Graphs must be numerically accurate. Your graphs may replace numbers with pictures, but the underlying figures demand credibility. If complex relationships and technically sophisticated matters are represented, ensure that they are statistically sound. Such issues are outside the scope of this book; but introductory statistics texts are widely available.

Maintaining credibility

To establish and maintain your integrity, ensure that:

■ scale reflects the numerical information;

■ titles and labels describe the data;

■ money is adjusted for inflation; use standardized units;

■ consistent scale is maintained in a series of graphs: changing scale can confuse or deceive readers;

■ the differences in numbers, not distinctions in design, are emphasized;

■ numbers do not appear on graphs: emphasize the visual.

To sum up . . .

Graphs are a means of illustrating numeric trends and relationships. They are best at telling an explicit story dramatically. They are better at broad points than fine detail.

Be sure your graph has a specific message, and use that message in your title.

When examining data during the discovery stage of your work, you may wish to try out a number of graphs. Later you can construct graphs to explain your message. When you present your graph publicly, it should no longer be a puzzle, but should tell a clear story.

The best graphs enjoy four major features:

First, they have a clear and specific message. Readers immediately understand their point, which is stated in the title. Your choice of data, of the story you wish to tell, makes the difference between a good and bad graph.

Secondly, successful graphs benefit from simple design. The type of graph chosen should be uncomplicated—and never three-dimensional or oddly shaped. All chart junk should be deleted, including grid lines, patterned bars, busy backgrounds, shading, and data labels. Graphs should take up no more than one-third of a page or screen and preferably much less.

Thirdly, the best graphs use clear and simple labels. Poor wording is a common cause of incomprehensible graphs. Labels need to be succinct, horizontal, and large enough to read. Label bars, lines, and pie slices individually. Avoid abbreviations unless commonly known. A summary discussion should always be included.

Finally, successful graphs possess integrity of intention and action. Many people are suspicious of graphs and statistics. It is more common to mislead people by accident than by design, but it is better not to mislead at all. Communicate honestly by listing your sources, making scale evident, and ensuring that your work is statistically valid and presented in context.

5 Using graphs

Introduction

Graphs excel at showing broad trends and relationships, at demonstrating what is big and what is small.

Bar graphs are good at showing relationships between different quantities, and line graphs are good at measuring changes in a series, usually time. These two graphs tend to be more successful—to communicate with more ease—than other graphs. Pie charts, scattergrams, superimposed graphs, and picture graphs are useful in a few limited cases.

Checklist for choosing the right graph

✔ useful	✔✔ excellent			
For data showing	Recommended chart			Notes
	Bar	Line	Pie	
Parts of a whole	✔✔		✔	
Changes over time	✔	✔✔		Line charts excel at showing changes over time.
Comparisons	✔	✔		Comparing two or more pie charts is not recommended.

56

Bar graphs

Bar graphs represent figures through bars or columns. They compare differences between two or more sets of numbers. You can use bar graphs to:

- compare different quantities: the cost of loans from different banks or the number of nurses in various European countries;

- show changes over time (however, line graphs are almost always better at showing trends over time);

- show parts of a whole: divisions of a budget, sales figures from all branches, etc.

Example 5.1 A simple bar graph

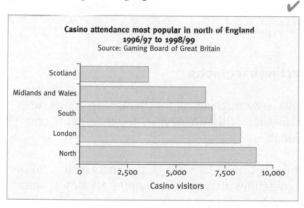

Bar or column?

Bars may be placed horizontally or vertically, in which case they are called columns. Horizontal bars are easier to label, and more bars can be shown down the side of a graph than across its base.

Some people find it logical to show speed and distance horizontally through bars, and to show money, and other measures associated with 'up' and 'down', through columns.

| Example 5.2 A simple column graph

This column graph is a version of the bar graph in Example 5.1.

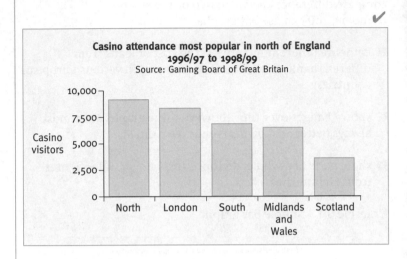

Constructing bar graphs

Bar graphs have much going for them. Most adults can understand them; they are easy to design and can look professional.

To design, label, and place bar graphs successfully, follow the general guidelines discussed in Chapter 4. Below is some specific advice on designing bar graphs:

■ Use bars of equal width and varying lengths. Unequal widths create optical distortions, causing readers to misunderstand the relative values.

■ Order bars by size. It helps the reader see relationships quickly.

■ Label clearly.

Ordering bars by size

If you organize bars from large to small it helps the reader compare the bars quickly. It has all the advantages of ordering numbers in a list or table and gives the graph a more professional and thought-out appearance.

Example 5.3 Ordering bars by size

The first graph is arranged alphabetically. The eye must adjust to the variety in bar lengths. Rearranged by size (as in the second graph), relationships are immediately apparent. These graphs contain the same data as in Example 2.1.

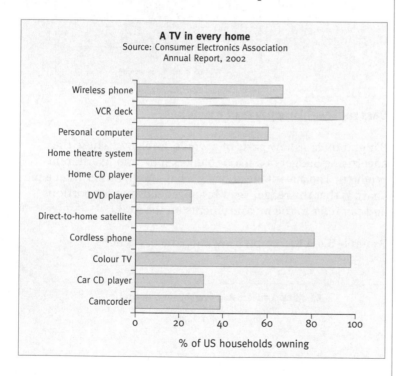

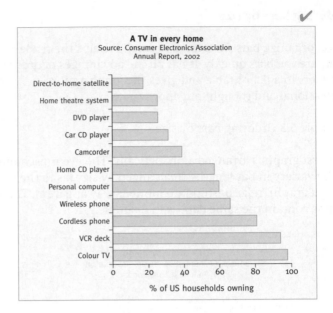

Bars representing parts of a whole

Bar graphs can show parts of a whole, as below, where the advertising budget of a major bank is split among different products. The advantage of using a bar graph, rather than a pie chart, is that the reader readily apprehends the proportions and can refer to the measurements on the axes.

Example 5.4 A bar graph showing parts of a whole

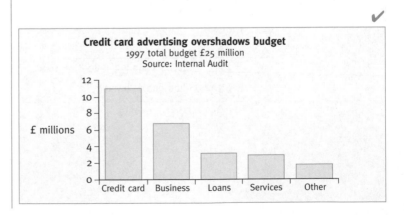

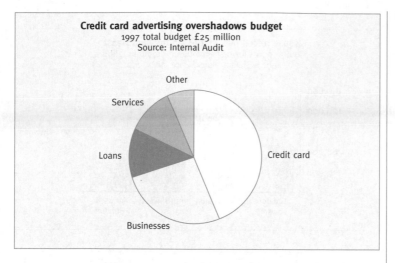

Paired bar graphs

Paired bar graphs (sometimes called grouped bar graphs)
compare two or more coupled items. You can use them to
contrast males and females, two time periods, pollution in two
cities, etc. Paired bar graphs can bewilder some users: after all,
you are looking at the data in two different ways. Readers may
puzzle over what information to compare. Good titles and
summaries can help compensate for these problems.

The principle is that information to be compared should be
physically close.

Example 5.5 Paired bar graphs

The paired graphs below compare house prices for first-time
buyers by both years and regions in England. In the first graph,
the primary category is the region and the sub-category is the
year. In the second graph, the year is the primary category and
the sub-category the region.

Paired and overlapping graphs can distort information and may be confusing. Keep your message simple and test samples on friends.

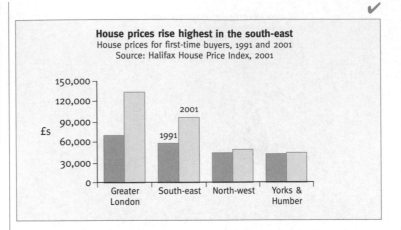

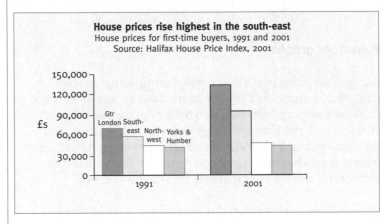

It is crucial to choose the right primary category for paired bar graphs. When organized by locale (as in the first graph above) readers focus on comparing regions—London is most expensive; only minimal differences separate the north-west from Yorks and Humber—and how prices changed over the period. The trends are easy to spot: more costly areas also saw the greatest increases in prices.

When the primary category is years (in the second graph) the graph is less successful. The reader has to study the graph to discover the trends. Data to be compared needs to be close.

Component bar graphs

Component (also called subdivided or stacked) bars consist of two or more segments. Like paired bar graphs, they have sub-categories. Like pie charts, they are used to show parts of the whole.

Component bars rarely justify themselves; they are not well suited to any single message. In addition, they easily distort data. There is so much information packed into a component bar graph that it is hard for it to communicate with ease.

When the lower segments of a component bar graph vary in size—as they usually do—the upper segments begin on different levels. The sizes of the individual segments become difficult to detect and comparisons distorted. Even with a definitive title, the graph is likely to remain a puzzle to the reader.

Example 5.6 Component bar graph

The message in the bar graph below is obvious only because of the title. The irregular lengths obscure comparisons. If this data merits presentation, it would be better displayed as a table or perhaps as a nine-bar graph.

A component bar graph has parts of a whole stacked on top of one another. A paired bar graph has components of a whole plotted side by side.

Component bar chars share similar problems with layered line graphs, see page 69.

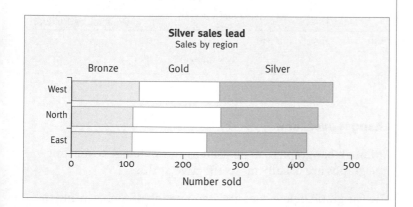

Negative bars

Bar graphs are capable of carrying negative information such as financial losses and negative percentage changes. With a definitive title, these charts can be made clear to most audiences.

Example 5.7 Negative bar graph

Labelling always presents a problem with negative quantities. Listing the bars by size and including a succinct title helps readers follow the message.

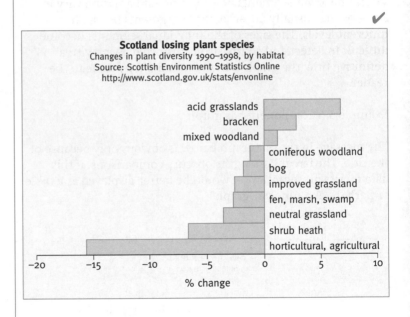

Scotland losing plant species
Changes in plant diversity 1990–1998, by habitat
Source: Scottish Environment Statistics Online
http://www.scotland.gov.uk/stats/envonline

Changes over time

Although bar graphs can be used to show changes over time, line graphs are usually more effective at this.

The bar graph below does an adequate job of representing the data; but only when the data are presented as a line graph do the trends become alive. With the line graph, you can quickly track the changes over the period.

Example 5.8 Bar graph over time

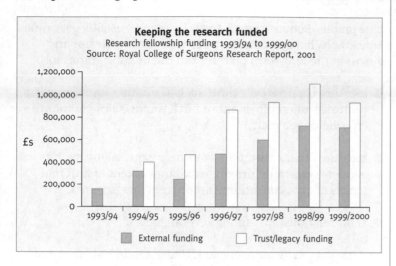

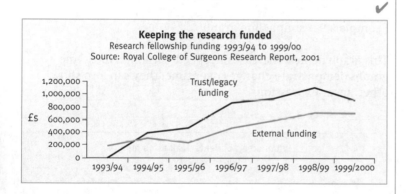

| # Line graphs

Line graphs demonstrate changes in a series, usually over time. Line graphs have a great ability to show flow—the ups and downs in the long-term picture. You can use line graphs to:

■ measure changes over time, such as minutes, months, years, centuries, unemployment or birth trends, sales per month, crop yields per year;

■ measure other continuums or linear expressions, such as accidents per miles driven, maximum speeds of different makes of cars, educational attainment and earnings;

■ show relationships among several figures.

Line graphs can be quite elegant. Understanding them is easy and creating them is straightforward.

Example 5.9 A simple line graph

This graph depicts increases in speed. Although most line graphs demonstrate changes over time, they can also show other linear expressions.

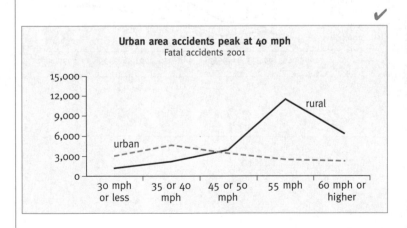

Constructing line graphs

Design, labelling, and placement of graphs follows the general guidelines discussed in Chapter 4. Line graphs especially rely on:

- a limited number of lines. Keep to five or fewer lines. More lines clutter the graph. If you have more than five lines, try combining categories or use a bar graph or a table.

- sufficient data to demonstrate a pattern; two or three points are not enough.

- distinct labelling. Place labels on the lines, not within a legend key. A legend key is too far removed from the dynamic action of the lines.

Little-known fact: French philosopher René Descartes developed the idea of using horizontal and vertical lines with scales in 1637.

How many lines?

Example 5.10 Too many lines

The graph below suffers from an overload of lines. The reader must concentrate to trace any single line. Comparisons require more effort than most people will give. The graph is too crowded for labels, but a legend only makes the reader work harder to decipher the meaning.

By dividing the training suppliers into three categories, you can reduce the number of lines, as shown in the second example. The graph is further improved by labelling each line individually. Note that the combined categories required an increase in scale from 600 to 2,000.

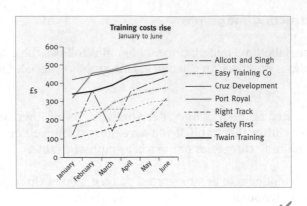

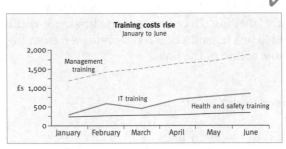

Example 5.11 Too few lines

Too few lines do not make a good graph. This is because graphs excel at showing trends, and two data points do not establish a trend. Line graphs only work with four or more data points. If you have only one or two numbers, simply put them in your text. For three or four use a table.

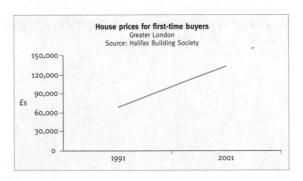

Layered line graphs

Layered line graphs (sometimes called area line graphs) are often seen in newspapers and textbooks. They share all the problems of component bar graphs. Because the segments are piled on top of one another, the shape of the upper categories is distorted. Line graphs that combine into layers sacrifice comprehension for showmanship.

Example 5.12 Layered line graph

This graph layers the data presented in the second graph in Example 5.10. There is nothing gained in using layers and only confusion is added.

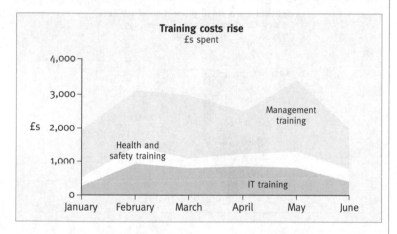

If you use a layered line graph, place the layer with the steepest slope at the top and that with the least slope at the bottom. That should reduce some of the distortion. Even if this rule is followed, readers may misinterpret the comparisons.

Pie charts

Pie charts show parts of a whole in a circle. No points for guessing why it is called a pie chart. You can use pie charts to:

Little-known fact: Florence Nightingale popularized pie charts in her arguments for better healthcare for soldiers during the Crimean War. William Playfair from Scotland invented the pie chart in the early 19th century.

■ show parts of a whole by percentages, such as the breakdown of a budget, percentage of households living in bungalows, etc.;

■ emphasize how a few components make up the whole.

Example 5.13 Simple pie chart

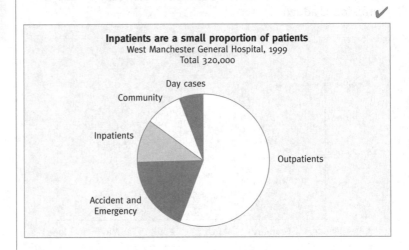

Inpatients are a small proportion of patients
West Manchester General Hospital, 1999
Total 320,000

Pies or bars?

Pies demand you compare quantities in a circle, when most of us think linearly. It is easier to compare lengths of bars or columns along a straight line than slices of pie in a circle. Despite their mass popularity, pie charts do not communicate well. Specialists in visual literacy, as well as many statisticians, avoid them.

On the positive side, people seem to like pie charts, so we offer some advice on designing and presenting them. Understanding the disadvantages of a pie chart will help you use them as effectively as possible.

Constructing pie charts

Constructing pie charts is relatively straightforward. Follow the general guidelines set out in Chapter 5. To use pie charts successfully:

- Give some idea of volume or quantity. Add this in the title so the reader will understand the size of the whole.

- Limit slices. Pies work best with five or fewer slices. More than five crowd the graph.

- Arrange slices in an order, usually from largest to smallest, beginning at 12 o'clock. This helps readers understand relationships. Most software programs do not do this automatically; you have to reorder the data to achieve such a size order.

- Avoid comparing two or more pie charts with each other. Though popular, these twin pies just compound the problem of comparing information contained in a circle.

Most software programs allow you to pull out a piece of pie to emphasize a particular point. This highlights the selected piece, but can disrupt comparisons.

Example 5.14 Limit the slices

Pie charts are best when showing a whole divided into five or fewer parts. For clarity, each pie slice needs an individual label. Too many labels hinder comprehension.

Help the reader by labelling each pie slice individually.

In first graph, the nine slices make the data almost useless. You could substitute a key legend, but the reader would have to flick from pie slice to the legend and back again. Legends add muddle, not clarity.

The second, revised graph combines categories and the graph becomes easy to understand. If you can't combine slices, consider using a table or bar chart.

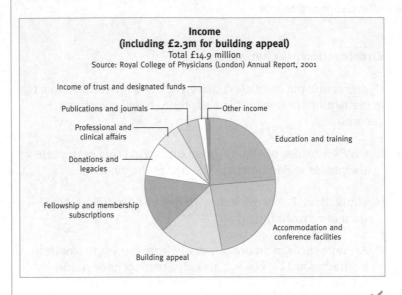

Income
(including £2.3m for building appeal)
Total £14.9 million
Source: Royal College of Physicians (London) Annual Report, 2001

Income of trust and designated funds

Publications and journals

Professional and clinical affairs

Donations and legacies

Fellowship and membership subscriptions

Building appeal

Other income

Education and training

Accommodation and conference facilities

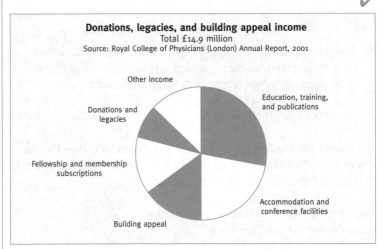

Donations, legacies, and building appeal income
Total £14.9 million
Source: Royal College of Physicians (London) Annual Report, 2001

Other income

Donations and legacies

Fellowship and membership subscriptions

Building appeal

Education, training, and publications

Accommodation and conference facilities

Remember that graphs should be vivid, making an immediate visual impact. Multiple categories drain the image of impact.

Comparing pie charts

Newspapers and advertising often present two or more pie charts side by side for comparison. Try to avoid this. Comparing slices within a single pie is difficult enough without expecting the reader then to compare data from another circle.

Example 5.15 Comparing pie charts

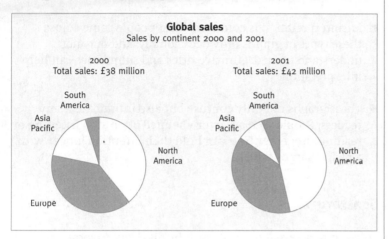

These two pie charts have been placed side by side supposedly for easy comparison. However, their differences need to be studied. Splitting the data between two charts makes it more difficult to read and understand. Comparative pie charts are a puzzle for the reader to work out. They communicate only with effort.

A simple table (see below) gives more information and more detail. As is often the case, numbers are more vivid than two graphs.

Sales by continent, 2000 and 2001, £ millions

	North America	Europe	Asia Pacific	Rest of world	Total
2000	15	15	6.4	1.9	38
2001	19	16	3.8	2.5	41

Figures have been rounded so sums may not total.

Other graphs

Bar and line graphs satisfy most needs for the visual display of data. Three other types of graph—scattergrams, superimposed graphs, and picture graphs—merit some attention.

These graphs are less common because they are less versatile and more intricate. Two points to consider:

■ Misinterpretation is common. Most people come across these types of graphs only occasionally, and may not understand them. Definitive titles and summaries can help interpretation.

■ These graphs not only confuse but also intimidate many readers. People who are overwhelmed often stop listening or reading altogether. You can hold their attention longer with a plain chart or table.

Scattergrams

Scattergrams reveal relationships by displaying a large number of individual points. They resemble line graphs because they are plotted on horizontal and vertical axes.

The technical aspects of scattergrams are outside the scope of this guide. If you need to know more, we suggest you consult an introductory statistics book.

You can use scattergrams:

■ during the discovery stage of your work to identify trends and relationships. After you have drawn your conclusions you can decide on the best presentation, which may be in another format such as a table or a line chart.

■ for large amounts of data. Scattergrams often show hundreds of data points.

Scattergrams demonstrate how numbers relate, rising positively or falling negatively. The technical term for this is *correlate*.

Data points that suggest a diagonal line from bottom left to top right indicate a positive value. A line from top left to bottom right indicates a negative relationship.

Example 5.16 Scattergrams

The first chart below demonstrates a positive correlation: the sale of fans increases along with the temperature. Note that the scattergram shows the full range of data, including points outside the primary trend.

The second shows a negative correlation between rising temperatures and the sale of heaters. The final scattergram demonstrates no correlation between sales of television and weather.

Scattergram 1: Positive correlation: fan sales increase as the temperature increases.

Data points? Each item is given a point on the scattergram according to the horizontal and vertical axes. These are called data points.

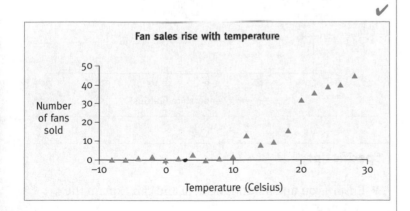

Scattergram 2: Negative correlation: sales of heaters decrease as the temperature rises.

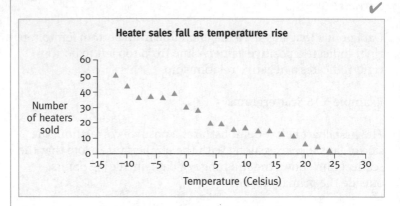

Scattergram 3: no apparent correlation: sales of portable televisions are not related to temperature.

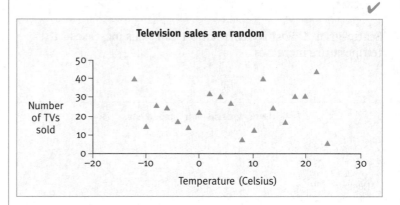

Specific tips

■ Ensure you understand the data and can explain the scattergram.

■ Label each axis clearly.

■ Include an explanatory title and summary.

Superimposed graphs

Superimposed graphs show the relationship of two sets of data working to two separate scales. Commonly they are a combination of bar and line graphs, but occasionally two lines with separate scales are used.

Superimposed graphs are most helpful at the discovery stage of your work. They can help you identify relationships in the data.

Example 5.17a A superimposed graph

A major disadvantage of superimposed graphs is that the two axes can easily be confused. The lines must be labelled carefully or they will remain a mystery to readers. Also, proper labelling of superimposed graphs on popular software programs is difficult.

Axis/axes? See the
Glossary for help.

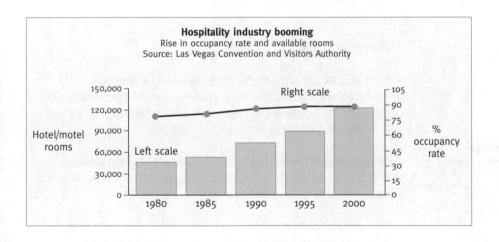

Hospitality industry booming
Rise in occupancy rate and available rooms
Source: Las Vegas Convention and Visitors Authority

Placing two graphs side by side is often more effective, as we show below. The *Economist* magazine—famed for its excellent presentation of data—often adopts this method of comparing items with two scales. By using two small graphs, relationships are clear and labelling is unambiguous.

Examples 5.17b and c

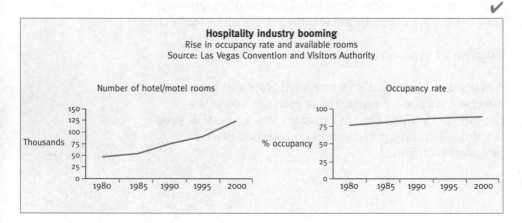

Pictographs

Pictographs are bar graphs with pictures or symbols representing quantities, for instance cows to represent milk production, or houses to represent house building. They are also known as isotypes and picture graphs.

Isotype
(International System of Typographic Picture Education) developed by Otto Neurath in the first half of the 20th century.

Pictographs are often seen in newspapers and magazines. Editors perceived them as an inviting way to show hard facts, such as military expenditure and tax increases.

Pictographs can be used to compare different quantities or compare changes over time, like ordinary bar and line graphs.

Example 5.18 A simple pictograph

Hallamshire ambulance service compared to similar areas

Source: Hallamshire Health Authority Annual Report, 2001

Artists sometimes argue that pictographs are more appealing than plain graphs. In fact, few graphic artists study, or have an understanding of, how to communicate specific information, such as statistics. If your graph has information that interests its audience and it tells a specific story, it should generate attention.

Have faith in your data. Decoration is just decoration.

To design pictographs, you need to:

- specify the value of each symbol, e.g. one ship stands for 1,000 oil tankers, one human figure for 10,000 people.

- choose symbols carefully. Does a red post box communicate postal services throughout the EU? Is the image large and clear enough to be seen as a VCR rather than a DVD player, an amplifier, or a shoebox?

- avoid inappropriate images, e.g. men for people, a cross for all religions.

- organize symbols horizontally rather than vertically. We are accustomed to reading horizontally.

If your statistics are boring, then you've got the wrong numbers.

Edward R. Tufte

Scale matters

Scale is a particular problem with pictographs. As we have seen with layered bars and lines, 3-D graphs, and odd shapes, images can deceive the reader.

Pictographs should compare data by showing different quantities of the same-sized symbol, as shown in Example 5.18. They should never use a single symbol of different sizes. There are two reasons for this. First, readers will not necessarily understand the relationship between the sizes. Secondly, to be accurate, the symbols must be proportional to the data and it will take you a long time to get the proportions right.

Example 5.19   Pictographs distort proportion

The data represented below are the same as in the pictograph above. The images vary proportionately to the data. However, few people can estimate the relative proportions and these comparative sizes are difficult to perceive. As with all area and volume images, interpretation is open to error.

Hallamshire ambulance service compared to similar areas

County C

County B

County A

Hallamshire

Source: Hallamshire Health Authority Annual Report, 2001

Illustrated (pictorial) graphs

These cousins of pictographs decorate graphs while adding no content. Illustrated graphs uses pictures as ornament and, like most gratuitous additions, these detract from meaning. They are popular in newspapers and magazines but it is doubtful if they actually assist people in understanding the figures.

To sum up . . .

Graphs are best at showing broad trends and relationships. Bar and line graphs are more successful than other types of graphs at communicating numeric ideas.

Bar graphs can be used to compare quantities, show changes over time and parts of a whole. Horizontal bar graphs are easiest to label and look professional when set in size order. Paired bar graphs compare groups of items and thoughtful organization of the pairs is essential. Similarly, component bar graphs compare two or three items and their sub-categories, but tend to be misinterpreted.

Line graphs are the best choice for showing changes over time but can also be used for showing changes in other linear expressions. To communicate with ease, line graphs should have five or fewer lines and each line should be individually labelled. Layered line graphs are similar to component bar graphs; they may contain too much data to communicate with ease, and can be misinterpreted.

See Chapter 6 for when to use a table and when to use a graph.

Pie charts show parts of a whole in a circle. Although pie charts are common and popular, experts believe they are difficult to use, and try to avoid them. When creating a pie chart, state the overall quantity represented. Limit pie slices to five or fewer and label each slice individually. Presenting two pie charts side by side makes both charts difficult to read.

Scattergrams, **superimposed graphs**, and **pictograms** are less common and also more difficult to interpret than the other graphs. They are useful in a limited number of circumstances.

Scattergrams show the relationship between many points on a graph. They can be useful during the discovery stage of your work. Superimposed graphs show data in relation to two different axes on the same graph. Two separate graphs side by side are likely to be a more successful way to compare such data.

Pictographs (and illustrated graphs) replace bars and columns with pictures or symbols. Although popular, they can distort the data and should be used with care. If you have the right data for your audience, the chart should not need decoration. The data alone will be interesting.

6 Table or graph?

Introduction

The choice between a table or graph should be based on your data and your purpose. When deciding on any table or graph, bear in mind the needs and expectations of the audience. Tables and graphs have different traits, which complement certain kinds of data.

Tables excel at showing a large number of items, exact figures, and a wide range of figures. On the other hand, graphs surpass tables for displaying dramatic comparisons.

See also Chapter 3, Using tables, and Chapter 4, Introducing graphs.

Use a table for
Precise numbers
Large amounts of numbers (reference material)
Comparisons
Parts of a whole
Great range between the largest and smallest figures

Use a graph for
Trends and relationships
Changes over time

Comparisons
Parts of a whole
Explaining a point vividly

Tips

■ If in doubt, use a table. Tables are more versatile.

■ Producing a table is quicker than producing a graph.

■ Do a quick sketch of your table or graph and see what it looks like before investing time on your computer.

Illustrate trends with graphs

Graphs excel at showing trends. Although tables give more detailed information, graphs can animate the information. The graph and table below present the same information. The graph shows the trend more vividly than does the table and provides more helpful information for health service planning.

Example 6.1 Use graphs to show trends

Emergency medical admissions persons aged 85 years or older,
West Manchester General Hospital, 1997–1999

	1997/98	1998/99
April	36	41
May	71	65
June	60	63
July	63	80
Aug	44	62
Sept	52	73
Oct	74	73
Nov	62	65
Dec	85	72
Jan	87	87
Feb	79	68
Mar	84	73

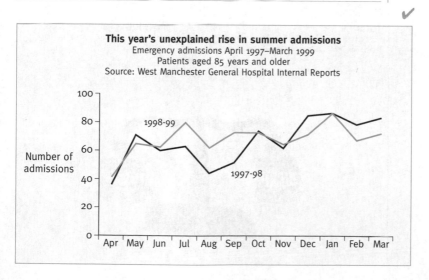

This year's unexplained rise in summer admissions
Emergency admissions April 1997–March 1999
Patients aged 85 years and older
Source: West Manchester General Hospital Internal Reports

Use tables for a range of numbers

Tables are best at showing actual figures and a wide range of figures.

Example 6.2 Use tables for a wide range of figures

In the example below, the number of staff in the education department overwhelms the graph, making it difficult to see any distinctions among the smaller departments. The table displays greater detail and, in part by using the natural shape of numbers, readers can see the relationship between the departments.

✔

Table 6 Staff per department, April 2002
Port Royal District Council numbers

Education	7,900
Social services	2,300
Housing	740
Leisure and recreation	690
Refuse and recycling	610
Construction	500
Libraries, museums and galleries	390
Planning & economic development	210
Environmental health	190
Others	560
Total	14,000

Figures have been rounded so sum may not total.

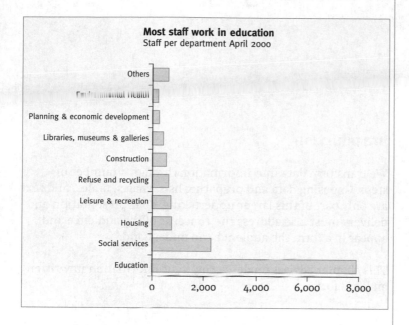

Most staff work in education
Staff per department April 2000

To sum up ...

Before choosing between a table and graph consider your information, your purpose, and the audience.

Use graphs for demonstrating trends and relationships. Use tables for presenting a wide range of figures and the precise numbers.

Part B contains a checklist for choosing a table or graph for your data.

7 | Presenting data

Introduction

We transform data into information through a number of
steps. Choosing data and preparing lists, charts, tables, and text
are only part of this larger undertaking. Your presentation and
delivery must also address the concerns of the audience and
appear in a form the audience can understand.

This chapter advises on delivering your information in written
and oral form.

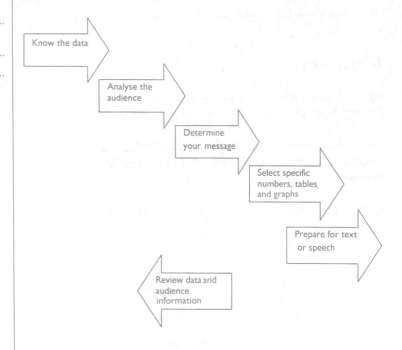

Know the data

Analyse the
audience

Determine
your message

Select specific
numbers, tables,
and graphs

Prepare for text
or speech

Review data and
audience
information

Audience and purpose always shape the presentation of information. The selection of the data, language, and the choice of table or graph are influenced by the context in which you are working. Think about how you might address citizens at a public meeting, executives in a briefing report, professionals at a conference, and the general public in a marketing campaign. In each case, language and data need to be tailored to make your point with that group.

Assess the audience

Putting the audience first may strike you as topsy-turvy—a more common approach is to think about the presentation after choosing your data and preparing the material. The problem with the usual approach is that the audience is an afterthought. Too often information is designed to meet the desires of the presenter, not the needs of the audience. Such an approach won't help your reputation or the audience.

Make sure your message is appropriate for the audience. A talk on cancer could be interesting to doctors, to patients' self-help groups, and to the local Women's Institute. But the language, knowledge, familiarity with numeric information, and expectations all differ.

To analyse your audience, ask yourself:

- Who will read or listen to this material? Why are they interested in the subject?

- What is their knowledge of the subject? What kind of detail do they need?

- Are they familiar with tables and graphs?

- For a written report, will it be read in a rush or more leisurely? On-screen or in hard copy? Readers tend to scan web pages and print out material they want to study.

- For an oral presentation, how much time are you allotted? What can you sensibly cover within that period?

■ What questions will the audience have? What decisions are they facing? Is there resistance to the position you present?

■ Some audiences are more formal than others. Some have greater technical knowledge. Get the style right.

Informal research can pay big dividends. Look over previous reports and ask how they were received. Question colleagues and co-workers about the audience for meetings and conferences.

One thing all audiences have in common is the need for tables and graphs that emphasize the information. Everyone— academic economists and school leavers, company directors, taxi drivers, and speakers of English as a second language— appreciates lucid and purposeful writing. Similarly, everyone appreciates unambiguous and meaningful data.

When addressing a knowledgeable audience, technical language and abbreviations may be appropriate. On the other hand, jargon (language that excludes part of your audience) is inappropriate. A group of highly qualified auditors may not know how to interpret a table on land planning if it lacks clear labels.

Determine your message

Once you have analysed the audience, you need to consider what you want to say to them and the best way to say it. You can communicate well only if you know your message.

Design for the medium. Print, computer monitor, and presentation software are discussed in Chapter 8.

The message is determined with reference to both audience and data. Review and adapt your data according to what you have discovered about the audience. When developing your presentation, you may wish to revisit the discovery stage of your work.

If you are presenting information on nutrition and cancer to the different groups mentioned above, your overall message to all of them would be to encourage a healthy diet. But with physicians, your purpose could be to alert them to nutritional factors that affect their patients (you might select data from studies on the biochemistry of nutrition and the direction of current laboratory research). For the support group you want to encourage good self-care (you could use evidence about remission and quality of life). For the Women's Institute, you emphasize diet as a predisposing factor and rebut some common myths (you might rely on public health information and translate research findings).

By honing the message, you will get a clear idea of what data to select.

After you have analysed the needs of your audience, you need to develop your message, choosing data that explains your subject or contributes to your position.

Select specific numbers, tables, and graphs

Once you define your message, you can choose and organize the appropriate figures. Your data should:

- compare;

- illustrate cause and effect;

- be timely;

- be accurate.

Use the Checklist for tables in Part B of this book.
Use the Checklist for graphs in Part B of this book.

Compare

When you use numbers, compare. Compare to last year, or to last century, or to Norway, or to your competitors, or to common expectations. Comparisons make numbers relevant, but pick relevant comparisons.

The sentence on the left below gives some information, but we don't know if the number of accidents is high or low. By introducing comparisons—as shown on the right—the information becomes more relevant and easier to understand and use.

In 2002, 23 accidents were reported at the Derby branch of the Winnipeg Track & Tool Company.

The Derby branch reported 23 accidents in 2002. This was 10% less than the previous year and well below the 50 plus accidents reported by the Halifax branch.

Illustrate cause and effect

Showing cause and effect makes numbers exciting as well as helpful. Reasons and results make up the stories that numbers tell. If you include figures in your work, they must somehow contribute to your overall purpose. Consider the logic in this report from a retail store:

A second rainy, cold summer in Belfast has reduced our sales of sun cream by 12%. A positive result was that umbrella sales increased dramatically.

The relationship should be established not coincidental.

Be timely

Use the most up-to-date figures you can get. Sales figures from sixteen years ago will not persuade anyone—last quarter's figures might. Sometimes getting timely figures takes extra effort, but it does make your work more persuasive, vital, and pertinent.

Be accurate

Are the figures accurate? Nothing can kill your credibility quicker than unreliable figures. (Rounded figures are accurate, as explained in Chapter 3.)

Most of us work with secondary data that was gathered elsewhere. It may come from surveys, government publications, newspapers, the stock exchange, and company reports. If you are working with other people's numbers, tailor the message to the audience through your selection and presentation.

Remember, you must credit the source and not distort the information.

Proximity and simplicity

The remainder of this chapter suggests guidelines for organizing and presenting information in text (on the page or screen) and speech. In both cases, proximity and simplicity are essential.

Proximity

Numbers need to appear as close as possible to explanations. This applies to oral presentations as well as written text. Listeners find it easier to link items if they are close. Compare the following:

Average house prices in Barnsley have increased by 15% during the quarter. This contrasts with Keighley, where houses now cost an average of £86,000 and there has been an increase of 3% in the quarter. It also contrasts to Selby, where the quarterly increase was 38% and the average house price is now £120,000. So the average price of a house in Barnsley is now £67,000.

Source: HBOS plc

✔

During the last quarter, average house prices increased in Keighley by 3%, in Barnsley by 15% and in Selby by 38%. At the moment, the average price in Keighley is £86,000, in Barnsley is £67,000 and in Selby is £120,000.

The example on the left is difficult to follow. The reader or listener can't easily compare house prices or percentage increases. The example on the right organizes the material into two lists, by percentage and by numbers. It allows more convenient and coherent comparisons.

Simplicity

Too many figures in a paragraph make laborious reading. Short tables and lists can take over from your text and speech.

The first paragraph below presents seven figures, in addition to years. Readers can't grasp and compare these different numbers.

In 2001, 35 million people visited Las Vegas, up from the 30.5 million in 1996. During this period, convention delegates increased by 500,000 from 3.3 million to 3.8 million. Most tellingly, hotel/motel rooms increased to 130,000 in 2001 from only 99,000 five years earlier.

In the second version, words and table are integrated. The introductory statements sum up the message. The second sentence sets the stage for the table.

The Las Vegas hospitality industry grew significantly from 1996 until 2000, as seen in Table 7.1. Visitors and convention delegates increased by 15%; hotel and motel room occupancy increased by 33%.

✔

7.1 Tourist figures, Las Vegas, 1996 and 2001

| | Millions of tourists | | Hotel/motel rooms occupied |
	Visitors	Convention delegates	
1996	30.5	3.3	99,000
2001	35.0	3.8	130,000

Source: Las Vegas Convention and Visitors Authority
Figures have been rounded so sums may not total.

Writing about numbers

Numbers appearing in written text—in sentences and paragraphs—are as important as those isolated in tables or represented in charts.

Newspapers, magazines, and book publishers have five centuries' experience of presenting figures. Common practices have grown out of this experience and, unconsciously, we are accustomed to these practices. These conventions make written work more readable and look professional. Below we set out some of these conventions.

Digits or words?

■ Spell out numbers one to ten. Begin digits at 11. This is a printers' convention and will be familiar to readers. The exceptions are decimals and fractions, for example 8.5 and 8½.

" This graph shows clearly that the woolly mammoth population has in fact been declining for years."

■ If a series has numbers above and below ten, use digits for consistency (*1, 6, 14* rather than *one, six, 14*).

■ Mixing words and numbers in a single concept helps readers see distinctions, for instance, *nine 6-inch rulers*, and *three 5-a-side football games*.

■ Use digits for most units of measure: *7 grams*, not *seven grams*; *6 inches*, not *six inches*, etc. Years are the exception, both *eighty years* and *80 years* are acceptable.

■ Readers prefer sentences that start with words rather than figures. *Seventeen monkeys were captured* is easier to absorb than *17 monkeys*… Alternatively you can recast the sentence to avoid the problem: *Yesterday, 17 monkeys were captured.*

Language

Write in plain English, using ordinary words. This keeps the readers' attention on your message, not your sentence structure. For instance, *per year* is preferable to *per annum*; *per person* is preferable to *per capita*.

See Jo Billingham's book *One Step Ahead: Editing and Revising Text.*

Decimals, fractions, and percentages

Consistent use of decimals or fractions in a paragraph helps the reader make comparisons, For instance, 2.5 and 7.25 fit together, as do 2½ and 7¼ . But 2½ and 7.25 makes comparison difficult.

To reassure readers they have not missed anything, add a nought, or zero, to decimals lower than 1, for instance, 0.88 not .88.

There is controversy over using % or spelling out *per cent*. Most newspapers tend to use the % now, but in more formal reports, spelling out is traditional.

Large numbers

Many people freeze when seeing large numbers. We can best reduce the use of large numbers through rounding and titles (e.g. *All sales figures are in thousands*).

- In text, add commas to long numbers. It is easier to understand 230,000 than 230000.

- Select *m* or *millions* and *b*, *bn*, or *billions* according to your context and audience. These abbreviations are well known. Both *million* and *m* (*£42 million* and *£42m*) are acceptable, as are *billion* and *bn* (*£52 billion* and *£52bn*).

- Avoid *k* for thousands (as in *£38 k*). The abbreviation *k* may be popular, but it is still unfamiliar to many people. Writers in a hurry will accidentally jot *£38,000k* for *£38,000*.

Rounding always helps large numbers. So £38 *million*, or £38.4 *million*, is easy for most people to grasp. But £38,413,000 and £38.413 *million* confuses many people.

Statistical language

Statistical information is comprehensible when put plainly, usually as a direct proportion. Most people understand *32 disabled children per thousand*, but can't envision *0.032 thousand disabled children*. Avoid statistical constructions, except for specialized audiences.

Accountancy terms

Two points when presenting financial data:

First, use chronological order. Some annual accounts are presented with the most recent period to the left of the previous period. For instance:

2002   2001

This is unhelpful to many readers who anticipate chronological order. 'First things first' is more logical and friendly to readers.

Secondly, use minus signs. In a list of figures, show negative numbers as *–350*, rather than in brackets, *(350)*. Few people are taught that brackets mean minus at school, but everyone knows what *–350* means. Brackets read like jargon; they are a barrier to easy communication.

Pictures versus information

In drawing up reports you may be under pressure to use tables and charts like pictures, to break up the page. The belief is that this makes publications more inviting and friendly. The principle is, of course, that you should only use a table or chart when the message dictates such a display. However, we appreciate that the practice of using graphs and tables to break up a page will continue, so offer this advice:

Use the opportunity to your advantage. Use data that is interesting, supports your overall point or argument, and is likely to be remembered. We suggest you:

■ identify data relevant to the audience;

■ appreciate that by including a table or chart people may look at that and not your words;

■ use demonstration rather than reference tables.

Speaking about numbers

Most people find numbers abstract; they don't seem connected to anything concrete. Hearing numbers spoken aloud (rather than reading them) makes understanding even more difficult.

Don't expect your listeners to follow a number-laden talk. Write down figures whenever you can: use overheads, slides, flipcharts, and whiteboards for the audience to see. Equally important, prepare and distribute simple handouts. A great number of people grasp numeric information by making notes. Without a handout, many of them will be busy writing down the numbers on napkins and agendas and won't listen to your point.

Tips

General advice on presentations is outside the scope of this book. We offer the following recommendations, which are specific to numerical information:

See Jo Billingham's book *One Step Ahead: Giving Presentations.*

■ When planning your presentation, imagine how it will sound to your audience. Stick to relevant figures and keep explanations direct. Write down the numbers.

■ Pause to give listeners time to absorb the figures. They won't be taking in new information while studying the numbers.

■ If you must use several figures (including dates), separate them, keeping the comparisons close. In the left hand example below, inserting the year and 2% in the middle confuses the comparison. By starting with the year and putting the percentage in a separate sentence, the idea is made clearer.

	✔
Average annual wages in Public Services, Administration and Defence in 1999 were £21 thousand (a 2% increase) and £18 thousand respectively for men and women.	*In 1999, annual wages in Public Services, Administration and Defence averaged £21 thousand for men, but only £18 thousand for women. Males enjoyed a 2% increase from the previous year.*

■ Use rounded figures. Their simplicity makes them memorable. Remember, most people cannot recall more than two digits.

	✔
1999 wages in Public Services, Administration and Defence averaged £21,123 per year for men, but only £18,303 for women.	*1999 wages in Public Services, Administration and Defence averaged £21,000 per year for men, but only £18,000 for women.*

'Four score and 7.33 years ago . . . or 87.33 years, or just over 85% of a century ago. . .'

Explaining a table or chart

Clarify and interpret any tables and charts you present. Show the table or chart on a handout or screen. Then follow these steps:

State the title.

↓

Explain the headings and the scale.

↓

Briefly summarize or interpret the table or chart.

↓

Give the audience time to read and take in the information.

↓

Ask for questions about the table or chart.

To sum up . . .

Knowing your audience and their needs is essential to delivering professional reports and presentations. There are specific considerations when presenting statistics, tables, and charts to the public.

Keep four basic concepts in mind when presenting data: the need to compare, the value of showing cause and effect, timeliness, and accuracy.

Construct your sentences and paragraphs with numbers in mind. Figures should be close to the words that explain them. Too many numbers in a sentence or paragraph is confusing to readers and listeners.

Practical conventions have grown up around using numbers in text. These help people communicate numeric ideas successfully. Particular advice exists for large numbers in text.

In writing and speech, reduce the number of figures mentioned whenever possible (while maintaining accuracy), and separate groups of figures.

Most people find listening to numbers spoken much more difficult than seeing them. Our advice is to show the numbers whenever possible. Always walk listeners through the titles, headings, and meaning of tables and charts.

8 Using technology

Introduction

Computers have transformed graphics, making the creation
and presentation of tables and graphs commonplace.
Word-processing, spreadsheet, and graphics software (such as
Word, Excel, and Adobe Illustrator) enable computer users to
produce numeric information that is both valuable and
striking.

The advantage of such software is its efficiency, power, and
prevalence. The popularity of tables and graphs suggests, in the
long run, an increase in numeric literacy. The disadvantages lie
in the predetermined formats that seem designed to
trumpet the program's capacity rather than to present
numbers according to any standards. Users are left with
many choices but no guidance. In the short run, we
may have more graphics but not necessarily improved
communication.

If you work extensively with tables and graphs,
it is worth mastering both a statistic package
(for instance, Origin 6.0, SYSTATA, SAS, SPSS)
and a graphics program, such as Adobe
Illustrator. This combination of statistic and
graphic software will produce the finest,
book-quality graphs, but demands investment
in time and money.

Einstein wrote the
Theory of Relativity
without the latest
top-of-the-range word
processor with
graphics package.

If you are working with a popular spreadsheet, such as Excel,
you can produce good tables and graphs only with rigorous
editing and deletion; you must ruthlessly remove features that
the program provides.

Recommendations for creating tables

Successful tables are easy to read and understand. We suggest using the Insert Table icon on the toolbar to build your own, clutter-free table. For simple tables we recommend that you:

- adopt single spacing. This locates comparative figures near one another. In long tables inserting a blank space every four or five lines helps readers keep their place.

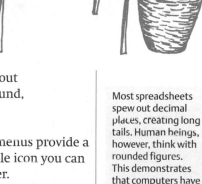

- align column headings to the right, like the numbers. Most spreadsheet programs position headings to the left and numbers to the right. This confuses readers.

- delay rounding to the last step. If you round earlier in your process and then carry out more calculations you are likely to double-round, creating errors.

Most spreadsheets spew out decimal places, creating long tails. Human beings, however, think with rounded figures. This demonstrates that computers have information, but no judgement.

- use the Format and Table functions. Format menus provide a choice of font and type size. Through the Table icon you can hide grid lines and sort numbers into an order.

Example 8.1 Creating simple tables

The first table below, produced by the standard Table Auto Format in Microsoft Word, is cluttered. It inexplicably emboldens numbers, and inserts pointless grid lines that steal attention from the data.

The second table was created through the Insert Table function, common to word processors. Its simple design—narrow, single-spaced, and no bold—emphasizes the data rather than the design.

Top ten UK house price hotspots, third quarter, 2002, average price

	Region	2001	2002	% change
Loughton	South-east	170,000	300,000	75
Smethwick	West Midlands	56,000	94,000	68
Pontypridd	Wales	51,000	85,000	65
Alfreton	East Midlands	51,000	82,000	62
North Shields	North	71,000	110,000	60
Wrexham	Wales	73,000	120,000	60
Whitley Bay	North	81,000	130,000	55
Wallsend	North	45,000	69,000	55
St Leonards on Sea	South-east	87,000	130,000	55
Taunton	South-west	120,000	190,000	54

Source: Halifax House Price (Regional) Index published by HBOS plc
Figures have been rounded so sums may not total.

Top ten UK house price hotspots, third quarter, 2002

City	Region	Average price		% change
		2001	2002	
Loughton	South East	170,000	300,000	75
Smethwick	West Midlands	56,000	94,000	68
Pontypridd	Wales	51,000	85,000	65
Alfreton	East Midlands	51,000	82,000	62
North Shields	North	71,000	110,000	60
Wrexham	Wales	73,000	120,000	60
Whitley Bay	North	81,000	130,000	55
Wallsend	North	45,000	69,000	55
St Leonards on Sea	South East	87,000	130,000	55
Taunton	South West	120,000	190,000	54

Source: Halifax House Price (Regional) Index published by HBOS plc
Figures have been rounded. so sums may not total

From spreadsheet to table

Excel and similar spreadsheet programs organize masses of numbers efficiently. They primarily function as worksheets, and need to be amended, reduced, and reorganized to become coherent tables for readers. This takes some effort, but combines the advantages of spreadsheets and standards of plain figures.

Some people set up spreadsheets to plain figures standards so that these are transferable straight into reports.

When transferring data from spreadsheets, check the following:

■ Does the table design follow the rules of plain figures?

■ Are titles and headings readable?

■ Can you reduce the amount of data? (The existence of data doesn't necessarily make it pertinent.)

■ Did you lose any of the data in transfer?

■ Have you reorganized the rows and columns, if necessary?

■ Are the tables placed immediately before or after any summary or explanation about them?

Recommendations for creating graphs

As explained in Chapter 4, we create graphs both to help discover the meaning of the data and later to explain its point to others.

During the discovery stage, you can experiment with the graph functions in word-processors and spreadsheets to see if interesting relationships emerge. Computers allow us to preview the data.

To build up your understanding of good tables and graphs, keep cuttings and print-outs of examples from magazines, newspapers, and the Internet.

However, software programs make assumptions about how data is plotted and graphs are displayed. The graphs in most popular programs spew out legends, grid lines, colours, values, and other effluvia. They offer dozens of choices, most of which promote junk at the expense of the message. See Chapter 5 for a full discussion of chart junk.

Become familiar with your program and use its facilities to maximum effect. Get to know chart functions, which allow you to delete borders, change shading and size, label and reorder bars or pie slices. Use the Help Index and look at your graph through Print Preview while designing it.

Example 8.2 Modifying software graphs

The following two bar graphs show the same data, but the second has been improved: it is free of grids and other lines, and of superfluous shading. The figures on the x-axis are not too large. The useless legend box has been deleted. Paradoxically, simplicity has to be worked for.

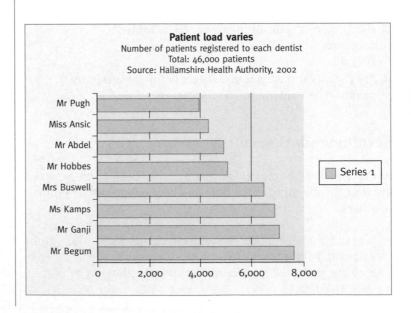

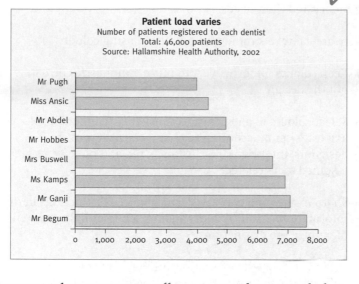

Patient load varies
Number of patients registered to each dentist
Total: 46,000 patients
Source: Hallamshire Health Authority, 2002

You must take numerous small steps to produce a graph that communicates with ease. It gets easier with experience. In general, follow these guidelines:

■ Stick to the simplest graphs in your program.

■ Learn how to label bars, lines, and pie slices individually. In some software, you must add 'values' to each item and then change the values to the desired label.

■ Wording should be horizontal and large enough to read.

Persevere: creating legible and informative graphs is sometimes time-consuming, but your payback is that people will understand the numbers and your message.

Colour

Colour is a key identifier throughout our lives. We perceive objects of the same colour as similar, regardless of shape, size, purpose, and location. Colour can animate design; it can also be overused and misused.

When creating graphs or other illustrations, colour is an important consideration. It has culturally specific meanings—in the west, red indicates danger or passion, but in China, it signifies happiness. Colours often vary on different computer monitors. To use colour well you need to think about your audience and their needs.

Here are a few recommendations about using colour:

■ Keep colours unobtrusive and mute. Emphasize the data, not the design.

■ Select colours in a logical and consistent manner. People associate items according to colour regardless of the designers' intentions. For instance, red and pink items are assumed to be related.

■ Sharp images and contrasts can reinforce distinctions in the information. Strong colours against white or light grey will maximize the distinctions.

Look at the bar graphs in Chapter 5 to see how black and white work effectively.

■ Some 5–10% of the population suffers from colour vision deficiency (colour blindness). Distinctions of colour—say slices on a pie chart—are lost to them. Sharp contrasts (for example light, dark, light again) will help.

Although colour brightens up graphs, reports, web sites, and presentations, it has limitations. It does not photocopy well and many people cannot make colour distinctions. Because of this, colour should not be the only identifier of bars, lines, or pie slices.

Finally, the impact of colours differs with the medium. Information on each medium is given below.

Presenting in different technologies

Every presentation medium—print, computer monitor, and presentation software—carries distinct features. Tables and graphs transfer between mediums only with distortion. Tables and graphs need to be created specifically for the medium in which they will appear. Remember that your primary task is to communicate the data.

Print

Print has been the standard method of written communication for centuries and most of us work better in print than in other medium.

Here are two tips for using paper to its maximum effect:

■ Construct tables and graphs with photocopying in mind. Colour copying costs more. Black and white photocopying of coloured graphs can lose vital information. Also, people sometimes reduce the size of the page when photocopying, making labels difficult to read.

■ Documents that will be distributed as email attachments or through programs such as Adobe Acrobat will be affected by the recipients' technology. Even page sizes differ. To guarantee a good standard of presentation, keep your graphics simple.

Computer screen

Computer screens hold less information than paper. Tables and graphs to be shown on web pages and CDs should be designed with this in mind.

Screens need to be simple. Clutter is a major problem on web pages, creating confusion and putting off the readers. Consider the home page for the Google search engine. Users immediately understand its purpose and how to proceed. Google's simple elegance contributes to its popularity over competing sites such as Excite and Yahoo.

A few suggestions to consider while designing web sites and CDs:

■ Fit tables and graphs onto a single screen. Scrolling is not an acceptable alternative. Viewers need to see a whole table for it to be meaningful. Successful graphs rely on their visual punch to communicate. Screens that demand scrolling miss the big picture.

■ Stick to 'web-safe' colours. These are a collection of over 200 colours that remain consistent on all operating systems.

■ As with paper, contrasts must be sharp and obvious. Unlike paper, brilliant colours (white, yellows, violets, and greens) can be contrasted against a dark background on computer screens.

■ Select a simple background that shows your graphics to advantage. It will also bring out your text.

■ Integrate graphics with text. Links to other pages are acceptable, but repeat the title on each new screen to maintain context.

Presentation software

Screens produced by presentation software (such as PowerPoint) resemble those on computer monitors. The major difference is that an audience watching a presentation cannot control the screen. That control lies with the presenter, who needs to be as unambiguous as possible while communicating the information.

Handouts

You can distribute handouts showing full versions of tables and graphs shown on screen. Such handouts are good practice. The handout should stand alone as a document appropriate for people who have missed your presentation or who wish to refer to it in six months' time.

Example 8.3 Handouts should be self-explanatory

Make handouts self-explanatory. The slide on the left below makes little sense to anyone who has not attended (or has forgotten) the talk. The slide on the right makes sense even to people who haven't attended.

- 1776
- 1789
- 1918

Dates of major revolutions

- 1776 USA
- 1789 France
- 1918 Russia

Here are some additional suggestions on using presentation software to show tables and graphs successfully.

■ Don't overload your slide with information.

■ Select fade-ins, animations, and sound conservatively. Ensure they complement your message. For example, a graph could develop from the static past to the projected future. Be careful that such tricks reinforce your content, rather than distract from it.

See Chapter 7 for suggestions on how to explain tables and graphs.

■ Reduce table sizes. Use 12 or 15 items maximum (3 rows and 4 columns; 5 rows and 3 columns). Remember, your audience has a very short time to absorb the numbers.

■ Make sure the text is large enough to read from the back of the room.

■ Explain each table or graph individually. Think of your audience and how they will receive the information.

■ Give your audience time to absorb the numbers. See the recommendations in Chapter 7 for talking about graphs.

■ Finally, explain your graphs as you go along. Think of your audience and how they will receive the information.

To sum up . . .

Computers offer great advantages in communicating numeric information. Unfortunately most computer programs provide decorative choice, but little assistance with good practices. Paradoxically, making tables and graphs simple can be more difficult than keeping them cluttered.

To create effective tables and graphs, you need to become familiar with your software program. Deleting borders, grid lines, and other distractions is often necessary. Treat spreadsheet data as raw information that must be adapted. Computers graphs allow us to experiment with data during the discovery stage and to display the refined visual dramatically for presentation.

With computers, colour is available and cheaper than it used to be. Sharp images and contrasts reinforce distinctions in images. However, differences in human perception, cultural association, hardware, and software must influence your selection of colour.

Paper, computers, and presentation software carry distinct and individual features. Each table and graph needs to be designed for the medium in which it will appear. For instance, the receiving computer may distort documents received through email.

Computer screens hold less information than paper, so information must be reduced. A plain background works better than a busy one. Presentation software shares most traits of computer screens.

To produce the most readable statistics, tables, and graphs, you need to be familiar with the program and the medium in which your work will be shown. Computers are only a bonus when the people using them exercise both knowledge and thoughtfulness.

Part B: Reference section
Contents

Checklist for tables

General

☐ Can you explain the purpose of the table?

☐ Is the table placed close to its summary or explanation?

Plain figures

☐ Are columns and rows ordered by size (or another system)?

☐ Are the numbers rounded to two digits?

☐ Are numbers to be compared in columns rather than rows?

☐ Have you provided focus through averages (or perhaps totals or percentages)?

Design

☐ Is the table structured simply?

☐ Have you used white space and bold lettering rather than grid lines for emphasis?

☐ Are numbers and column headings aligned to the right?

☐ Is the table situated correctly on the page?

☐ Are the tables consistent throughout the document?

☐ Is the table only as wide as necessary (and not artificially stretched across the page)?

Wording

☐ Is the table title comprehensive? Are the row and column headings succinct?

☐ Has someone else proofread the table?

Checklist for graphs

General

☐ Is the graph's message clear and memorable?

☐ Does it tell a single story?

☐ Does the title reinforce the point of the graph?

☐ Is the graph appropriate for the type of data?

Design

☐ Does the graph use the simplest design of its type?

☐ Is all chart junk removed? Be ruthless!

☐ Is the graph situated correctly on the page?

☐ Are the lines, bars, and pies directly labelled?

☐ Is the scale proportionate to the numbers?

☐ Is the graph less than a third of the page in size?

☐ Are the graphs consistent throughout the document?

Text

☐ Does the graph's title encapsulate its meaning?

☐ Is the text legible, horizontal, and in both upper and lower case?

☐ Is the written explanation as close as possible to the graph?

☐ Has someone else proofread the graph?

☐ Is all the necessary information given (subject, location, dates, units of measure)?

Checklist for placement and text of tables and graphs

Placement

- ☐ Is the table or graph placed close to the discussion in the text?

- ☐ Are tables and graphs aligned to the left or centred on the page?

- ☐ Are tables and graphs placed at the top or bottom of a page or screen (rather than in the centre, surrounded by text)?

- ☐ If several graphs are used, are they numbered, with a reference in the table of contents?

Text

- ☐ Does the title include sufficient detail to make the data comprehensible?

- ☐ Are titles and headings complete, giving all the necessary information?

- ☐ Does the text discussion or summary emphasize the meaning of the numbers?

- ☐ Is all language (including abbreviations) familiar to the audience?

- ☐ Is the text legible?

- ☐ Is the text in upper and lower case (rather than all capitals)?

- ☐ Are the sources listed?

- ☐ Has someone else proofread the graph or table?

Preparing data for a report

Work out your overall objective or purpose in presenting data.

↓

Consider your audience:
- familiarity with subject
- level of expertise
- technical knowledge
- commitment of time and effort

↓

Examine raw data for pertinent evidence, trends, and exceptions.

↓

Reduce raw data. Select specific figures that are
- relevant to your purposes
- appropriate for your audience

↓

Present your information
- according to the rules of plain figures
- in tables or graphs

↓

Adapt your material for
- print
- computer screen
- presentation software
- overhead projector screen
- handout

↓

Recheck tables and graphs:
- against the original data for accuracy
- with a colleague, friend, or editor to ensure others understand it

Further reading and resources

Books

A Primer in Data Reduction, A. S. C. Ehrenberg (John Wiley & Sons, 1982). Despite the offputting title, this excellent introductory statistics book contains several chapters devoted to communicating numbers. Beautifully written.

Plain Figures, Myra Chapman and Cathy Wykes (The Stationery Office, 1996). An in-depth book, with many fine examples.

The Visual Display of Quantitative Information, Edward R. Tufte (Graphs Press, Cheshire, Connecticut, 1983). Another excellent and beautiful book about displaying data. Although all Tufte's books are interesting, if you can only buy one book, buy this one.

The Non-Designer's Design Book, Robin Williams (Peachpit Press, Berkeley, California, 1994) Although not about communicating numbers, it offers valuable advice on principles of design for the interested amateur.

British Standard 7581, 1992: The Presentation of Tables and Charts (The British Standards Institute, 1992). The ultimate authority.

Say It With Charts, 4th edition, Gene Zelazny (McGraw-Hill, 2001). Several useful ideas about graphs.

Web sites

All web sites active at time of publication.

www.edwardtufte.com The discussion board, *Ask ET*, on this site offers an opportunity to get advice from a world leader in displaying quantitative information. The lively discussion ranges from production issues to Japanese animation. Always interesting.

http://www.dartmouth.edu/~chance/ *Chance* is a quantitative literacy course from universities in the United States. The web pages and the monthly *Chance News* focus on probability and statistics, not information graphics; but *Chance* offers an informative and entertaining site for learning more about how numbers work.

http://www.statistics.gov.uk/ National Statistics Online, the UK's official statistics site, contains a huge amount of information. Though the graphs are not as well designed as possible, the excellent tables can be downloaded.

http://www.statcan.ca/english/edu/power/toc/contents.htm *Statistics: Power from Data!* offers advice on collecting, selecting, and editing as well as presenting data. This site, nicely organized, and clearly written for the layperson, is from the government of Canada.

http://www.isixsigma.com/offsite.asp?A=Fr&Url=http://nilesonline.com/stats/ Robert Niles, a reporter for the *Los Angeles Times*, offers advice for journalists (who are famously innumerate). Sections on definitions, data analysis, and finding information.

CD-ROM

Visual Design for Instructional Multimedia, though targeted to education (kindergarten through college), is valuable for everyone. One of the few resources that documents the reasons behind recommendations. More information at http://www.extension.usask.ca/vdim/welcome.htm

Organizations

Plain Figures, PO Box 168, Wakefield, West Yorkshire WF1 3XD www.plainfigures.com Offers courses and consultation on all aspects of presenting figures.

The Plain Language Commission, The Castle, 29 Stoneheads, Whaley Bridge, High Peak, SK23 7BB. Courses and editing services on plain language.

Popular Communication Courses Limited, 60 High Street, Bridgenorth, Shropshire, WV16 4DX. www.popcomm.co.uk Courses in all aspects of writing and designing.

Case study: From raw data to useful information

The following case study tracks raw data through from discovery to final presentation. It involves exam results of a school and the different ways a head teacher might present them to the governing body. She will need to do some background work (the discovery stage) before finalizing the information (the presentation stage) for the governors.

The raw data comes to her in alphabetical order by subject:

1. Number of examination entries and grades

	A	B	C	D	E	F	Total
English	15	27	42	35	33	21	173
French	11	24	46	13	9	5	108
Geography	3	9	47	39	14	4	116
History	1	7	29	22	45	15	119
Maths	10	23	56	43	29	3	164
Science	22	34	31	33	21	12	153
Total	62	124	251	185	151	60	833

During the discovery stage, the head teacher will need to look at the data in different ways to get an idea of what it means. First she calculates the percentage of A to C passes for each subject. (In England, A to C grades are considered to be 'good passes'.) This is done in Table 2 below. Ordering the table by percentage exam success lets her quickly see performance by subject, while also showing the number of pupils entered per exam.

The head teacher sees that most exams have an A to C pass rate of between 49 per cent and 57 per cent. The exceptions are French with 75 per cent and History with only 31 per cent. There is no correlation between the number of pupils sitting an exam and good results. For instance both French and History have relatively few pupils taking the exam, yet the pass rate for French is high and History is low.

2. Exam results, 2002

In order of the highest percentage of A to C passes

	Number of passes						Total	No. of A to C passes	% of A to C passes
	A	B	C	D	E	F			
French	11	24	46	13	9	5	108	81	75
Science	22	34	31	33	21	12	153	87	57
Maths	10	23	56	43	29	3	164	89	54
Geography	3	9	47	39	14	4	116	59	51
English	15	27	42	35	33	21	173	84	49
History	1	7	29	22	45	15	119	37	31
Total	62	124	251	185	151	60	833	437	

The head teacher then creates a bar graph illustrating the distribution of A to F grades (Figure 3 below). It shows that the pupils are more likely to receive an E or F grade than an A or B grade. Like many graphs, it gives you less information than the table.

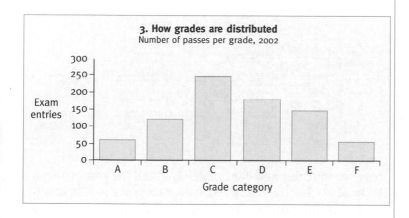

3. How grades are distributed
Number of passes per grade, 2002

To get a full picture of the school, the head teacher decides to compare the results with data from previous years. She constructs the following line graph (Figure 4), showing the improvement in the percentage of pupils gaining A to C grades.

Case study

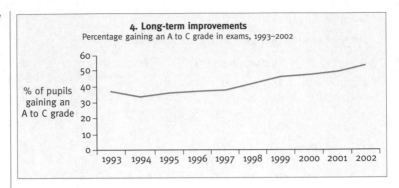

4. Long-term improvements
Percentage gaining an A to C grade in exams, 1993–2002

She also wants to compare the results with other schools. A bar graph (Figure 5) shows her that the school does not perform well compared to others in the local area.

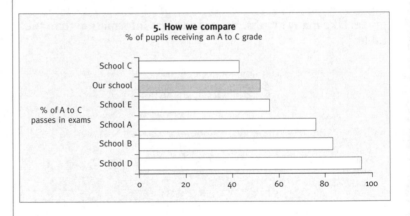

5. How we compare
% of pupils receiving an A to C grade

These separate line and bar graphs don't tell the whole story. The head teacher then looks back over six years and decides to compare improvement of schools. This information compares the trend from the line graph (Figure 4) and the bar (Figure 5).

When the head teacher sets out in a table the percentage change in A to C exam results over the past six years, another story is told. Suddenly we can see that our school has made substantial progress. In fact it is the most improved of the six schools.

This can be done in a table, as in Figure 6, or a graph, Figure 7.

6. Improvements over six years

	% of pupils receiving A to C grades		% change
	1997	2002	
Our school	37	52	15
School A	64	76	12
School E	53	56	3
School C	40	43	3
School D	97	95	−2
School B	86	83	−3
Average	63	68	

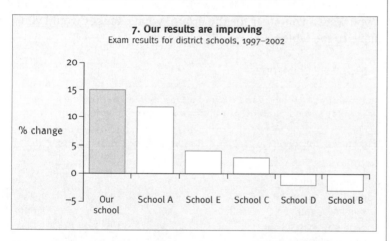

7. Our results are improving
Exam results for district schools, 1997–2002

In presenting the data to the governors, the head teacher would probably choose to show Figures 2, 4, 5, and 6 above. Although there is nothing wrong with the bar graph in Figure 7, the table—Figure 6—contains more information. She may use it for dramatic effect.

The head teacher writes her report, explaining each figure in her text. The report concludes that the teachers and pupils should be pleased that there has been a steady and impressive improvement over the period. On the other hand, more improvement is needed to match the standards provided by other local schools.

Exercises

The following exercises are designed for you to test your skill at using the ideas and principles set out in this book.

Suggested answers (there are no absolute answers) are listed at the end of this section.

Exercise 1 Presentation of numbers

The Friends of Canadian Libraries sponsored a contest encouraging communities to read a specific book in the summer of 2002. Here are part of the results, as posted on the Friends' web site (http://www.friendsoflibraries.ca/).

If you were a volunteer for the group, what changes would you make to the table?

The Chesley Challenge

Communities reading *In the Skin of a Lion* by Michael Ondaatje, by number and percentage of population (reproduced in part).

Registered library	Reading tally	% population reading	Population
Wolseley Branch Library, SK	43	5.059%	850
Tisdale Community Library, SK	55	2.967%	1,854
Chesley Area Public Library, ONT	70	2.500%	2,800
Bjorkdale Branch, Wapiti Regional Library, SK	5	1.923%	260
Welland Public Library, ONT	86	1.755%	49,000
Bruce County Library, Wiarton Branch, ONT	36	1.565%	2,300
Paris Branch, County of Brant Library, ONT	76	.844%	9,000
Cobourg Public Library, ONT	165	.750%	22,000
Mildmay Carrick Branch, Bruce County Library, ONT	6	.600%	1,000
Perry Township Public Library, ONT	12	.487%	2,465

Exercise 2 Patterns and exceptions

04 Exercises

This table shows the percentage of staff who replied 'yes' when asked if they were generally satisfied with aspects of their working conditions.

Staff satisfaction, August 2003: percentage of respondents

| | Branch | | | | |
	Bristol	Derby	London	York	Average
Health and Safety	75	78	73	73	75
Hours	88	90	79	87	86
Management	68	71	81	67	72
Parking facilities	76	84	69	12	60
Average	77	81	86	60	

(a) Reorder the columns and rows from largest to smallest by average size. What are the main patterns and exceptions in the data?

(b) Go back to the original table. Can you now see the patterns and exceptions?

(c) Can you suggest other ways in which the readability of this table can be improved?

Exercise 3 Improving readability

The following table has been drawn up to give senior managers data about sales. List ways in which the table's readability can be improved.

Value of sales orders by region and source, 2002 (£)

Received from	London and south	Midlands and Wales	Outside Europe	North	Europe	Scotland and Northern Ireland
Franchises	59,811	17,828	6,717	21,889	10,579	40,684
Agents	34,789	48,575	34,501	39,151	25,958	33,167
Website	10,654	18,586	10,297	10,704	7,059	11,290
Travel shops	8,180	7,682	5,455	7,526	4,512	9,809

25

Exercise 4 Proximity

This table was drawn up to help senior managers decide between employing either three or four whole-time-equivalent (WTE) youth workers.

(a) What major rule does this layout break?

(b) How can the table be improved?

Cost options for youth service		
3 WTE posts		4 WTE posts
6–13.2k	Office base/equipment (dependent on location, e.g. room in community centre) 6–13%	7.8–16.9k
3.55–4.1k	Volunteer/travel/study 3.5–4%	4.55–5.2k
6k	Stationery / telephone / fax 6%	7.8k
2k	Publicity / training 2%	2.6k
7–10k	Management fee (audit, payroll, etc.) 7–10%	9.1–13k
71k	Wages 70%	91k

Exercise 5 Fixed and variable rounding

Round the following numbers:

Original	Variable rounding to two effective digits	Fixed rounding to thousands
764,375		
23,694		
5,872		
438		
38		
11.3		

Exercise 6 Rounding to two digits

Round the following numbers using variable rounding.

Round to two digits

Series1   88,722
          54,114
          25,555

Series 2   504
            496
            494
            487

Series 3   9,811
            622
             89
           42.777
            5.388
            0.75577
            0.043844

Exercise 7 Mental arithmetic

Work out the difference between 437.96 and 661.42 without using a pen, paper, or calculator. Now compare 440 and 660 in your head.

Exercise 8 Table or graph?

Use the data below to plot a graph on a piece of paper. What does the graph tell you compared to the table?

% staff with	1970	1975	1980	1985	1990	1995	2000
No qualifications	92	84	76	62	54	47	37
Professional qualification or degree	3	6	8	15	26	32	53

1 Introduction

Exercises

Exercise 9 Three-dimensional graphs

The following graph, from a borough council tax demand, is meant to show the sources of council income.

What are the disadvantages in using this 3-D pie chart for this purpose?

Can you suggest a more effective way of presenting this information to the public?

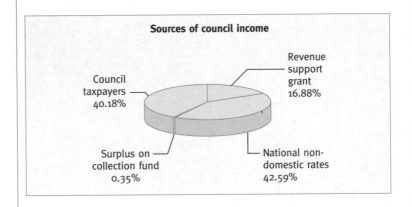

Sources of council income

Council taxpayers 40.18%

Revenue support grant 16.88%

Surplus on collection fund 0.35%

National non-domestic rates 42.59%

Exercise 10 Becoming familiar

Look through a selection of serious newspapers and magazines that use graphs. Examine the first five graphs you come across. Make a note of what the message is for each graph. Can you think of ways to improve the communication of the graph?

Exercise 11 Graphs

Match the appropriate graph with the following data:

1 Parts of a whole   A. Line graph

2 Changes over time   B. Bar graph

3 Comparing sizes or amounts of quantities   C. Pie chart

Exercise 12 Improving graphs

This graph is produced by the Food and Agricultural Organization of the United Nations. You can examine the multicoloured original at

http://www.fao.org/WAICENT/FAOINFO/ECONOMIC/ESS/chart/home.htm

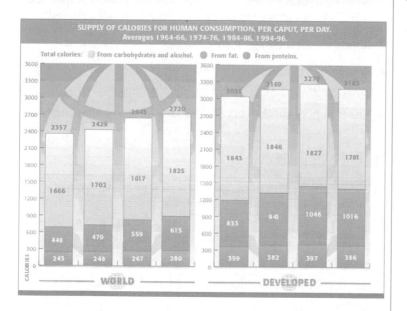

What type of graph is hidden under the chart junk?

List the different comparisons made in the graph.

What improvements are needed?

Answers

Exercise 1 Presentation of numbers

To improve the table:

■ Reduce the data: remove repetitive words like *county* and *branch*. Put other words, like *public library*, and the % into the title. The two Bruce County entries can be amalgamated.

■ Round the percentage figures and population figures.

■ Reorganize columns so that the percentage—the comparative measure—is the first column.

■ Insert blank spaces every four or five lines to help the reader follow the data.

The Chesley Challenge

Communities reading *In the Skin of a Lion* by Michael Ondaatje, by number and percentage of population.

Library	% population reading	Reading tally	Population
Wolseley Branch, SK	5.1	43	850
Tisdale, SK	2.9	55	1,900
Chesley Area, ON	2.5	70	2,800
Bjorkdale Branch, Wapiti Regional, SK	1.9	5	260
Welland, ON	1.8	86	49,000
Bruce County, ON (2 libraries)	1.2	42	3,300
Paris Branch, Brant County, ON	.84	76	9,000
Cobourg, ON	.75	165	22,000
Perry Township, ON	.49	12	2,500

The original was correctly organized by size.

The information could be improved further, depending on the purpose:

■ Smaller tables could focus on communities of 1,000 and less, towns of between 1,000 and 10,000, cities over 10,000.

■ Are all the columns necessary? A list of communities and the percentage of the population reading the book might suffice.

The Chesley Challenge

Communities reading *In the Skin of a Lion* by Michael Ondaatje, by number and percentage of population.

Registered Library	% reading	Reading tally
Wolseley Branch, SK	5.1	43
Tisdale, SK	2.9	55
Chesley Area, ON	2.5	70
Bjorkdale Branch, Wapiti Regional, SK	1.9	5
Welland, ON	1.8	86
Bruce County, ON (2 libraries)	1.2	42
Paris Branch, Brant County, ON	.84	76
Cobourg, ON	.75	165
Perry Township, ON	.49	12

Exercise 2 Patterns and exceptions

Once you have ranked the data numerically, spotting patterns and exceptions is easier.

Results of staff satisfaction survey, percentage of respondents

	Derby	Bristol	London	York	Average
Hours	88	90	79	87	86
Health and Safety	75	78	73	73	75
Management	68	71	81	67	72
Parking facilities	76	84	69	12	60
Average	81	77	76	60	

Most staff are satisfied with their working conditions, those in Derby being the most satisfied. Employees in York are the least satisfied, and are particularly dissatisfied with parking. A relatively high percentage of London staff are satisfied with their management.

Switching rows and columns will improve the readability further. Numbers to be compared should be close to one another because it is more likely that readers would be interested in comparing the opinions from different branches than different criteria.

Results of staff survey

	Hours	Health and Safety	Management	Parking facilities	Average
Derby	90	78	71	84	81
Bristol	88	75	68	76	77
London	79	73	81	69	76
York	87	73	67	12	60
Average	86	75	72	60	

Exercise 3 Improving readability

The readability of the table is improved by:

■ rounding to two digits;

■ switching rows and columns;

■ ranking rows and columns by size;

■ including averages.

Further, giving thousands in the heading makes the numbers simpler. The revised layout makes the patterns stand out. It is now apparently that agents are responsible for most of the sales, and out-perform other ways of selling in every region. Franchises, on the other hand, are disproportionately successful at selling in London and the south, and in Scotland and Northern Ireland. The web site has been more successful at selling to the Midlands and Wales than elsewhere.

A new title could stress the pattern.

Agents lead our sales
Value of sales orders by region and source, 2002 (£ thousands)

	Agents	Franchises	Web site	Travel shops	Average
London and south	35	60	11	8.2	28
Scotland and NI	33	41	11	9.8	24
Midlands and Wales	49	18	19	7.7	23
North	39	22	11	7.5	20
Outside Europe	35	6.7	10	5.5	14
Europe	26	11	7.1	4.5	12
Average	36	26	11	7.2	

Exercise 4 Proximity

Answers

The major rule broken is, of course, that data to be compared should be close to each other. In the original, the numbers are separated by text, making comparisons more difficult.

The table can be improved in a number of ways, including rounding the numbers to two digits, ranking by size, better labelling (avoiding the abbreviation WTE), introducing thousands in the title and deleting *k* from the table, and aligning data and column headings to the right.

Cost options for youth service (£ thousands)

	Whole-time-equivalent workers		% of total budget
	Three	Four	
Wages	71	91	70
Office base/equipment (dependent on location, e.g. room in community centre)	6–13	7.8–17	6–13
Management fee (audit, payroll, etc.)	7–10	9.1–13	7–10
Stationery/telephone/fax	6	7.8	6
Volunteer/travel/study	3.6–13	4.6–5.2	3.6–4
Publicity/training	2	2.6	2
Total	96–120	120–130	

Figures have been rounded so sums may not total.

Exercise 5 Fixed and variable rounding

Original	Variable rounding to two effective digits	Fixed rounding to thousands
764,375	760,000	764,000
23,694	24,000	24,000
5,872	5,900	6,000
438	440	0
38	38	0
11.3	11	0

133

Exercise 6 Rounding to two digits

Certain numbers cannot be rounded because they are too close numerically. Rounding them would introduce unacceptable rounding errors.

		Round to two digits using variable rounding
Series 1	88,722	89,000
	54,114	54,000
	25,555	26,000
Series 2	504	These cannot be rounded because
	496	they are too close numerically.
	494	Rounding them would introduce
	487	unacceptable rounding errors.
Series 3	9,811	9,800
	622	620
	89	89
	42.777	43
	5.388	5.4
	0.75577	0.76
	0.043844	0.044

Exercise 7 Mental arithmetic

The two amounts differ by 223.46. Was the time and effort involved worthwhile? Would the use of 220 (from your rounded calculation) rather than 223.46 (from the precise one) be meaningful for most of your use of numbers?

Exercise 8 Table or graph?

Even a rough line graph shows the story more vividly than does the table. Line graphs are more effective at illuminating the data than other types of graphs.

Simple graphs like this one communicate quickly and effectively.

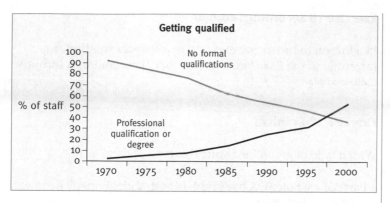

Exercise 9 Three-dimensional graphs

There are a number of problems with this graph. The intended audience has been forgotten, of whom many will have little experience in looking at graphs.

In any event, three-dimensional graphs are notorious for distorting images.

The pie chart is an especially poor choice because of the distortion among slices. Finally, taxpayers are unlikely to need data to two decimal places. A bar or column graph will not work here because of the large spread between 43,000 and 5,300,000.

It is possible to transfer some noughts to the title.

A short, uncluttered table will give the public more relevant information than any graph. Both rounding numbers and ranking by size dramatically improve readability.

Sources of council income	Net income	%
National non-domestic rates pool	5,300,000	42
Council taxpayer	5,100,000	40
Revenue support grant (central govt)	2,200,000	17
Surplus on collection fund	43,000	0
Total	13,000,000	

Figures have been rounded so sums may not total.

| **Exercise 10 Becoming familiar**

In addition to the magazines and newspapers you find, we recommend the *Economist*, the *New York Times*, and the (Toronto) *Globe and Mail*.

Exercise 11 Graphs

Which type of graph best suits this type of data?

1 Parts of a whole **B**. A bar graph is best, though many people would use a pie chart.

2 Changes over time **A**. Line graph.

3 Comparing sizes or amounts of quantities **B**. Bar graph.

Exercise 12 Improving graphs

A stacked bar graph lies under distracting shapes, lines, and numbers.

Once the chart junk is removed, we can see that the years (given in the title) need to be placed under each column and that the second y-axis label is unnecessary. Jargon terms such as 'caput' or 'per capita' can be replaced with 'per person'. Here is the same graph pared down:

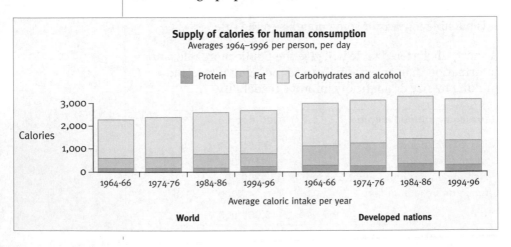

Supply of calories for human consumption
Averages 1964–1996 per person, per day

Apart from the chart junk, this graph suffers from multiple comparisons, including:

■ years (1964–6; 74–6; 84–6; 94–6);

■ world and developed world;

■ calories;

■ calorie sources (protein, fat, and carbohydrates).

There are too many comparisons to be represented successfully. The data could be organized into at least five effective charts:

■ world and developed world by calories source for 1994–6 period only (paired bar);

■ world and developed world by total calories for 64–6 to 94–6 (paired bar);

■ world by total calories and developed world by total calories by time period (line graph with two lines);

■ world by each calorie source by time period (line graph with three lines);

■ developed world by each calorie source by time period (line graph with three lines).

To create a readable graph from this data you must first decide what you want to say: you must reduce the data to a single message. Graphs are most powerful at telling a single story. When they try to cover everything, they communicate little.

Glossary

average

In common usage (and in this book) *average* stands for the arithmetic **mean** calculated by adding up items and dividing the total by the number of items.

axis

A fixed reference line in graphs. The horizontal line is called the **x-axis**. The vertical axis is called the **y-axis**. Plural is *axes*.

bar graph or graph

A diagram that displays data by comparing the height or length of bars of equal width. Bar graphs are usually horizontal. A vertical bar graph is called a column graph.

chart

A visual representation of data: see **graph**.

chart junk

Unnecessary decoration in graphs.

circle graph

Pie chart.

column graph

A vertical bar graph, which displays data by comparing the height of bars.

data

data

Facts and statistics collected together for reference or analysis. Data must be interpreted (usually through patterns); it is meaningless by itself. Formally, *data* is plural; the singular is *datum*. In practice, *data* has come to be used for both.

demonstration tables

Tables constructed around selected figures to illustrate a particular trend or message.

digit

Any of the numerals from 0 to 9, especially when forming part of a number.

figure

A number, especially one that forms part of official statistics or relates to the financial performance of a company.

graph

A diagram showing numeric relationships measured along a pair of axes at right angles.

grouped bar

A graph that presents pairs of bars.

information

Facts that have been organized into a meaningful form.

Isotype

A pictoral depiction of **data**. Isotype (International System of Typographic Picture Education) was introduced in 1936 by Otto Neurath, who proposed a system of picture characters as an alternative to written script. Though Neurath's system failed, Isotype is often used to mean **pictograph**.

key legend

The wording on a map or diagram explaining the symbols used.

linear

Able to be represented by a straight line on a graph.

line graph

A graph that compares two variables through a line.

mean (arithmetic mean)

The average of a set of numbers calculated by adding them together and dividing by the number of items.

median

A quantity lying at the mid-point of a set of ordered numbers; it is calculated by crossing off an equal number of entries from below and above.

mode

The value that occurs most frequently in a given set of numbers.

negative correlation

A relationship between values that plots as a downward slope on a line graph; as one value increases, the other decreases.

number

An arithmetic value, expressed as a word, symbol, or figure, representing a particular quantity and used in counting and making calculations and for showing order in a series, or for identification.

outlier

A data point on a graph that is very much bigger or smaller than the nearest point. Outliers are surprising, and may indicate an error or an important exception.

percentage

A rate, number, or amount in each hundred; any proportion or share in relation to the whole.

pictograph

A pictorial representation of statistics on a graph. Pictographs may repeat a symbol or change the proportions of the symbols to indicate numbers. In both cases, misinterpretation errors are prevalent.

pie chart

A type of graph in which a circle is divided into sectors that each represent a proportion of the whole.

positive correlation

A relationship between values that plots as an upward slope on a line graph; the two variables increase or decrease together.

ranking

A position in a scale; ordering of numbers from smallest to largest or largest to smallest.

scale

A standard system for measuring or grading something; a ruler-like measurement for the x- and y-axis of a graph.

scattergram (scatter plot, scatter diagram)

A graph in which data is plotted but the points are not joined into lines; the pattern of the points reveals any correlation.

statistics

Information obtained by collecting and analysing numeric data in large quantities.

table

A set of facts or figures systematically displayed, especially in columns and rows.

variable

Something that can change. Graphs contain at least two variables—numerical values—that are plotted on the x- and y-axis (e.g. age or number of people in a household).

x-axis

In graphs, the horizontal line.

y-axis

In graphs, the vertical line.

Index